I thoroughly recommend thi[...]

angst or self-doubt; women pl[...]

and flourish in their Christian faith. Easily accessible and written with warmth, its practical biblical wisdom will both challenge and comfort those who are struggling with emotional baggage and difficulties, yet long to mature as Christians.

Ann Allen
International speaker, Kilsyth, Scotland

This is a great book. Mary Whelchel, who has served as our director of women's ministries for many years, knows all of the hot-button issues that people find difficult to get over; so, whatever your hang up, it is almost certainly dealt with in this book. As a pastor, I've known far too many people who can't move on with God because they are bound by carefully nursed hurts that they refuse to put behind them. Read this book and then pass it along to others who need to quit wallowing in their past—no matter how terrible it might be—and unload the baggage they have carried far too long.

Dr. Erwin Lutzer
Senior Pastor, Moody Church, Chicago, Illinois

Mary, ever straightforward, practical and relevant, gives advice few have the courage to give. "Get Over It!" She boldly declares that each of us holds the key to those shackles that bind us: hurt feelings, comparisons, wrong attitudes, petty fears, discontent, fear and much more. She combines that practical "How to" that is her trademark, with fresh, biblical insights that are both inspiring and empowering. Thank you, Mary, for this much-needed book!

Miriam Neff
Author, Founder and President of *Widow Connection*, Chicago, Illinois

With the candor of a faithful friend, Mary Whelchel encourages us to get over our petty fears, attitudes and anxieties that prevent us from living freely and becoming all that God intends for us to be. Drawing on years of ministry experience, Whelchel provides practical advice and wisdom to fight our tendency to hold onto slights, guilt and unrealistic expectations. Time and again she points us to the truth of Scripture, exposing the fault lines in our thinking and reminding us that we are called to trust God in every area of our life.

Melissa Kruger
Author of *The Envy of Eve, Finding Contentment in a Covetous World*, Charlotte, North Carolina

What a relief to know we can get over hurt feelings, wrong attitudes, unrealistic expectations, and false guilt! These are just some of the issues that Mary Whelchel successfully addresses in *Get Over It!* She not only reminds us of the need to get over those things that drag us down and hold us back, but she also shows how we can do this by giving us tried and tested principles that we can put into practice right away. With its biblical foundation, personal illustration, and practical application, *Get Over It!* has what it takes to help you let go and move on with God.

Florence MacKenzie
Author of *Destructive Emotions: Facing Up to Guilt, Fear and Anger,*
Aberdeen, Scotland

So often it's the little things that mushroom in their power to bog us down, impede our progress, rob us of joy, and deplete our energy. Mary Whelchel draws from her own journey with God and her years of ministry to shepherd readers to the place of letting go of burdens we weren't meant to carry and courageously moving forward with God.

Carolyn Custis James
Author of *Half the Church,* Boxford, Massachusetts

Mary Welchel in her book *Get Over It* exposes for us our inward looking, self-promoting and desire to please others, and challenges us to be more Godward looking, God-promoting and desiring to please Him. She encourages us to 'Let go and let God'. An excellent book for all ages and stages in life. I wish that it was available when I became a Christian as it would have really challenged me to move forward and grow in Jesus. I would use this book in Bible studies as a tool to challenge people to move on and get over the hang-ups, because when the Son sets us free we are free indeed.

May Nicholson
Author and founder of Preshal Trust, Glasgow, Scotland

In *Get Over It*, Mary Whelchel shows women, in very practical ways, how to live free from dangerous mindsets that are so easily entangling. Mary gives women a gentle, yet powerful biblical approach to handling offenses, while continuing to walking in love, and total forgiveness. *Get Over It* is a much needed book in our culture today. *Get Over It* can serve as a powerfully resource for all women, church leaders, teachers, students, and all who consider themselves worshipers of the Living God.

Alicia Williamson Garcia
Author, Worship Leader, Conference Speaker, Mobile, Alabama

GET OVER IT!

LETTING GO AND MOVING ON WITH GOD

MARY WHELCHEL

CHRISTIAN FOCUS

Mary Whelchel is the founder and host of the radio programme, "The Christian Working Woman", heard on over 500 radio stations in the U.S. and internationally. She is a frequent speaker at retreats and women's events, and has authored many books, including *Extraordinary Women by Grace*, *Soaring on High*, *How to Thrive from 9 to 5*, *Think About What You Think About* and *Common Mistakes Singles Make*.

Copyright © Mary Whelchel 2013

paperback ISBN 978-1-78191-145-7
epub ISBN 978-1-78191-208-9
Mobi ISBN 978-1-78191-209-6

10 9 8 7 6 5 4 3 2 1

Published in 2013
by
Christian Focus Publications, Ltd
Geanies House, Fearn,
Ross-shire, IV20 1TW, Scotland
www.christianfocus.com

Cover design
by
Paul Lewis

Printed by
Bell and Bain, Glasgow

MIX
Paper from
responsible sources
FSC® C007785

CONTENTS

INTRODUCTION

There is a classic skit from the comedian and television star Bob Newhart that remains one of the funniest I've ever seen. Bob, who portrays a psychologist, invites a client into his office for consultation, and informs her that he charges $5 for five minutes, and he is certain that is all the time she will need. Of course, she is thinking she'll be there for an hour, and maybe for weeks on end, but he insists they'll be done in five minutes or less, and invites her to tell him her problem.

She confesses that she has a great fear of being buried alive in a box. He asks if anyone has ever tried to bury her alive in a box, and when she says no, he tells her he has two words for her. Two words that will solve her problem immediately. She is ready to take notes, but he insists she won't forget the two words. So, as she is poised to hear these incredible two words that will free her from this fear of being buried alive in a box, he looks at her and screams, "Stop it!"[1]

That's pretty close to my idea of counseling. However, my choice of words would be updated and expanded to three words: Get over it!

I know they're not soft, gentle, warm and fuzzy words. I know they seem to lack compassion and mercy. I know they sound abrupt and very simplistic. But I believe, mainly from my own experience with myself, that those are three words we simply need to hear and heed quite often. Honestly, I say them to myself regularly, as I find myself mired down in all kinds of joy-robbing thought patterns and unhealthy habits.

Like a pig to a mudhole, we keep going back to a place that gets us dirty, makes us unsightly and smelly, and keeps us from moving forward to the good things God has for us. Isaiah 43:18-19 is a passage of great hope:

> Forget the former things; do not dwell on the past. See, I am doing a new thing! Now it springs up; do you not perceive it? I am making a way in the desert and streams in the wasteland.

How often we miss the new thing that springs up because we can't get over something from our past. It could be the distant past or what happened five minutes ago, but these things become the mudholes of our lives where we wallow on a daily basis and never find the way in the desert and the streams in the wasteland.

There is certainly a place for long-term, in-depth Christian counseling for people, and I'm fully aware of

---

1   You can view this on YouTube at http://www.youtube.com/watch?v=BYLMTvxOaeE

that great need. In my position as director of women's ministries at my urban church, I am regularly dealing with women who need lots of help in order to move forward. We offer it in various ministries at our church and I often recommend a Christian counselor who has more education and understanding than I do about some emotional struggles.

But I am convinced that there are still many daily issues all of us face which don't really require a lot of advanced education or knowledge to deal with successfully. We simply need to get over it and remind ourselves to just stop it.

That's what I hope to address in this book, with some very practical wisdom I've learned in my twenty-eight or so years of ministry.

Chapter One

Get Over Hurt Feelings

She looked distraught as she came up to speak with me after a customer-service seminar I taught. Then she began to tell me her rather long story of an incident that had happened on her job. Choking back the tears, she told me how a customer had treated her rudely, abruptly, and condescendingly without provocation and for no reason. At first I expected to hear of some truly horrible episode, perhaps where she had been threatened or her job had been put in jeopardy. But the longer I listened, the more I realized that she was telling me about a one-time interaction with a rude customer, certainly not pleasant, but not uncommon when you're in a customer service job.

I asked her when this had happened, thinking it must have been raw—like yesterday! But no, as she scratched her memory to come up with a dateline, she said it had been probably eighteen months ago, perhaps two years.

Trying not to reveal my amazed reaction, I attempted to give her some advice that would help her get over it! But as she walked away, I didn't get the feeling that she really wanted to get over it. She simply had hoped for some sympathy, perhaps some confirmation that she was right and the customer was wrong. My "get over it" advice didn't seem to work. She had harbored those hurt feelings for months, daily re-living the pain this stranger had caused her, and was mired in misery as a result.

Why do we hang on to hurt feelings so long, thereby heaping unhappiness on our own heads? We certainly don't get any revenge on our offenders by hanging on to hurt feelings. If you think that a pity party will relieve some of your hurt, think again! Pity parties are addictive, as well as pitiful! The more you feel sorry for yourself and harbor those hurt feelings, the more you will try to find comfort in your self-pity. It can be a vicious cycle, and, of course, it only makes matters worse.

Pity Parties Are Pitiful!

Years ago God began to reveal to me how hooked I was on pity parties. And what came as a major revelation to me was that God sees it as a sin. Whether or not I have a legitimate complaint, wallowing in self-pity, nurturing my hurt feelings was not what a mature Christian should do. I wanted to grow up in Christ, to become more like Jesus, and I began to see how wrong and silly it was for me to insist on my pity parties.

I well remember the night I came home from work with my feelings hurt—again—by my insensitive boss. I was nurturing those hurt feelings by going over in my mind his hurtful words, what I wished I had said to him, what I would say to him some day, how unfair he was, ad infinitum. Instead of doing something productive, I plopped down to waste an evening by throwing another pity party, and pity parties are indeed pitiful since no one ever comes and there is nothing to celebrate.

As I began to indulge myself by feeling sorry for myself, I stopped and thought, *I don't want to feel sorry for myself. I don't want to be miserable. I will not throw a pity party tonight.* And with that I got busy, put those hurt feelings behind me, and got over it! It was a major turning point for me, as I began to learn that I didn't have to hold on to those hurt feelings. I could, by a set of my will with the power of God's Spirit, get over it.

Wouldn't it be wonderful if we could get over those hurt feelings from our past? I recognize that some hurts are extremely deep and painful, and may indeed need some time and help to relinquish. But let's just think about the little things that hurt our feelings in our normal, everyday lives— such as the example I shared with you at the beginning of this chapter. Here are a few that come to my mind:

- A person ignored me—didn't acknowledge he/she even saw me.

- A friend spoke to me in a very unfriendly tone of voice.

- My sister didn't call me for five days—and she knew I was sick.

- My boss didn't give me credit for an important project I completed.

- My husband didn't even notice my new hairdo.

- My close friend had a dinner party and didn't invite me.

There are so many small—even insignificant—things like these that hurt our feelings. Even as I write this, I've spent some time this day thinking about a slight affront I felt a couple of days ago. There I go again, allowing my feelings to be hurt unnecessarily, wasting valuable thought time, dwelling on the negative, and feeling offended! Get over it, Mary!

Perceived Offenses

Our hurt feelings are often based on inaccurate information and wrong perceptions. We misread something and allow it to hurt our feelings without checking it out. For example, if you pass a friend in a hallway—at work, church or wherever—and you expect her to notice you and speak to you, but she doesn't, you can feel offended because you think it was intentional. But if the truth were known, she might have a serious problem on her mind, or maybe she just got some very bad news, or she is trying to make a deadline—or any number of other situations—that have her so preoccupied that she truly did not see you.

You may think, "Yeah, but she should have seen me," and that may be true, but your perception is that she intentionally ignored you. You're thinking that she saw you, didn't want to speak to you, and chose to be rude and ignore you, and therefore your feelings are hurt.

I think these perceived offenses happen every day, and the person who takes them personally and reads into them some intended offense is bound to allow their feelings to be hurt regularly. Here's how you get over it:

- When you feel offended, stop and ask yourself, "Did she/he truly intend to offend me?" If the answer is "No" or "I don't know," then you should certainly get over it, put it out of your thoughts and refuse to let it back in.

- Put yourself in the other person's shoes and think, "I wonder if something is wrong?"

- Remind yourself that you do the same thing to others at times when you're preoccupied, and you need their understanding just as they need yours.

- Send up a quick prayer for her/him and ask God to meet their need at the moment, whatever it may be.

Exaggerated Offenses

Once we allow ourselves to be hurt by something that may be truly insignificant, our imaginations go to work and, given a little time, that small offense becomes a major one. Any time we dwell on negatives, we exaggerate them and they take on far greater importance than they merit.

I challenge you to become aware of your own tendency to exaggerate small offenses—or even large ones, for that matter. We are by nature very self-absorbed, and it is so easy for us to feed these offenses and allow them to grow into grotesque and abnormal experiences. I find this is one of my chief battles, and I have to continually stop myself from blowing things out of realistic proportions.

Some years ago I got a phone call from one of the women in my church, and out of the blue she apologized to me for having bad feelings toward me. She explained that two years previously I had said something rude to her on the phone, and for that reason she had stopped coming to my

Sunday class, talked against me, and basically didn't like me. God had convicted her that she had not handled it biblically, by coming to me directly when it had happened, and so she was apologizing.

To this day I have never been able to remember the offense, so I was stunned to hear her confession. Of course, I apologized for whatever I had done or said that had offended her, but I also pleaded with her to never again let anything like that go for two years, harboring the hurt she felt, when we could have settled it once and for all by talking about it at the time, when I might have been able to remember it, or just by letting it go.

I know that I never have held any bad feelings toward this woman, so whatever I had done or said was simply misunderstood by her, perhaps poor word choices by me, but nothing intentional. But for two years she had harbored this offense, exaggerated it way beyond anything realistic and endured pain as a result, while I suffered nothing because I had no idea that I had offended her and would have made it right immediately, had I known.

I'm glad to say that is all in our past, we're on very good terms again, and I think she learned a good lesson. You just can't hang on to these hurt feelings, because they grow and take on a life of their own!

Hebrews 12:15 says, "See to it that no one misses the grace of God and that no bitter root grows up to cause trouble and defile many." Hurt feelings turn into bitter roots, and those bitter roots grow up to cause trouble.

What Does Jesus Think?
What does Jesus think about our pity parties? Can you even imagine Jesus throwing a pity party? Can you

imagine Him talking or even thinking about how He had been offended? He expected trouble and offense in this sin-infested world, but it never caused Him to dwell on those offenses or harbor them.

What if this very day you had to stand before Jesus and explain the hurt feelings you are harboring right now? Would you ever say to Him:

Lord, I realize I could have gotten involved in that ministry and helped out there, but you see, my feelings were hurt. Jennifer said something to me that was very unkind, and how can I work with Jennifer when she has hurt my feelings. I'm sure you understand, Lord.

Lord, I would have done that for you, but you see, I was left out. Nobody invited me to be a part of it, so I just figured they didn't want me.

Lord, I know you didn't expect me to keep on doing that job after the way they treated me. Somebody else came on the scene and they did what I used to do. So, I wasn't going to hang around there and just let them walk all over me like that.

Lord, nobody ever said thank you or gave me any credit for what I did. So, you understand, there was no way I could keep on doing that.

Lord, I stopped going to that church because they were unfriendly. I could sit there for an entire service and nobody would speak to me. So, I just quit going. You understand, I'm sure.

Lord, I don't speak to that co-worker anymore because she never smiles at me, she never speaks to me, she acts like I don't exist. I can't be expected to speak to her, right?

17

None of us would have the nerve to voice these excuses to the Lord, would we? Well, have you forgotten that Jesus is right there with you at all times, hears every word you say, knows every thought you think and every attitude you hold, and is totally aware of the hurt feelings you are harboring? It's true that He sympathizes with us and shares our sorrows, but when we are weighed down with unnecessary hurt feelings, when we're stuck in our pity parties instead of moving into the new things He has for us, surely He must shake His head in regret that we can't get over these hurts. He knows better than anyone how they are robbing us of joy and peace and the abundant life He came to give us.

We really have to get over these kinds of hurts, don't you think?

How to Get Over Hurt Feelings
Here are six general principles to help you get over harboring hurt feelings:

1. Change your attitude about pity parties.
What I would hope is that you will get really fed up with pity parties, as you see how much damage they are doing to you and to everyone around you. Just get good and mad at the enemy who has used this weapon against you time and again. Ask God to give you holy anger about pity parties, to see them as He sees them, and to get sick and tired of feeling sorry for yourself.

2. Refuse to think about the bad reports; think only about the good reports!
I like this translation of Philippians 4:8:

Finally, brethren, whatsoever things are true, whatsoever things are honest, whatsoever things are just, whatsoever things are pure, whatsoever things are lovely, whatsoever things are of good report; if there be any virtue, and if there be any praise, think on these things. (KJV)

Usually when our feelings have been hurt, we are thinking about some bad report. It has helped me greatly to tell myself over and over again, when I'm tempted to feel sorry for myself, "Mary, stop thinking about the bad reports. Think about some good reports." I often start reading the mail from the listeners to my radio program, which helps me focus on the good things God is doing through our ministry. Those good reports will break up a pity party fast.

When you start to dwell on an offense, make yourself think of something positive about the person who offended you. For example, if your mate hurt your feelings this morning, and you're brooding over it and exaggerating it, think about the good things about your mate, the reasons you chose him/her to be your mate.

As soon as you become aware that you're dwelling on some perceived or real offense, replace that wrong thinking with thankful thoughts. Sing a song of praise. Recite all you have to be thankful for. Think of people you know who have really big problems and pray for them. Bring that thought into captivity and force it to be obedient to Christ.

We demolish arguments and every pretension that sets itself up against the knowledge of God, and we take captive every thought to make it obedient to Christ. (2 Cor. 10:5)

3. Resist the enemy who is trying to entangle you and hinder you by making you feel sorry for yourself.

Just say to the enemy, out loud if possible, "Sorry, but I'm not having a pity party today, so take off the party hat and go find someone else. I refuse to feel sorry for myself. I don't have time and I'm not wasting that energy." The Bible tells us that if we resist the enemy, he will flee from us.

4. Think about Jesus and all that He endured.

Hebrews 12:2 says, "Let us fix our eyes on Jesus..." By a set of your will, stop thinking about poor me, and think about Jesus; fix your eyes on Him. Think about how He suffered such awful indignity and pain for you, and you will be embarrassed to feel sorry for yourself when you compare your situation to His.

5. Get busy doing something constructive.

Don't just sit there; do something! This is one time you need to get involved in constructive activity that will take your mind off your hurt feelings and shut down that pity party. A friend of mine tells me that her great-grandmother would frequently say to her, "If you have time to feel sorry for yourself, then you don't have enough chores to do." As she puts it, "It is more difficult to 'wear your feelings on your shirt sleeve' when you're 'rolling up your shirt sleeves' and serving others."

6. If you have something against someone else, either go to them and get it out in the open, or put it behind you.

There are times when we need to go to the person who has hurt our feelings and get some issues out in the open. Here's a good suggestion: Write down on a piece of paper or type into your computer exactly what is bothering you, how your feelings have been hurt, and what you would like to say to that person. Then put that in a safe place for two days, and during those two days pray about what God would have you do.

After two days get the paper out or open it up, reread it, and ask for God's wisdom. If you still believe you should go to that person and settle this thing, then decide how to tell the truth in love, make sure you're not acting in anger or just self-interest, and then go to them at an appropriate time.

If you're not willing to do that, or it no longer seems that important, tear up that piece of paper or delete it from your computer and say to the Lord, "I'm putting this behind me; it is in the past and you will take care of it from this point on. I will, by your grace, get over it."

The worst thing you can do is to keep brooding about it. Either do something or get over it.

Again, quoting my friend, Marila:

> When you're hurt, do you listen well to the Holy Spirit? Or, are you so busy talking about your hurt that He doesn't have a chance to get a word in edgewise? Without a supernatural God-response to hurt, we often wallow in self-pity and embroider around the injustice, especially to our friends or family who will listen. Repeatedly talking about hurt only confirms, convinces, consumes, and sets the offense in concrete. In fact, injustice, like a fishing story, always becomes larger in the retelling.[1]

Life is too short for harboring hurt feelings. I beg you to "get over it!"

---

1   From *The Leader* newsletter, Volume 3, Issue 6, April 23, 2003, "What Hurts Your Feelings?" by Marila Palmer.

Chapter Two

Get Over
Comparing Yourself
to Others

After my freshman year in college I was traveling to Maryland from my home in Georgia to work for the summer as a counselor in a Christian camp. I had a twenty four-hour bus ride, as I remember, and during that long ride I made a decision to change my personality. I was going to a place where no one knew me, so I thought I had the perfect opportunity to be whoever I wanted to be.

I decided that instead of being the outgoing, assertive, take-charge type that I had been all my life, I would become the quiet, reserved, undemonstrative type of person. It seemed to me that this kind of personality was a much better one than the one I had—especially for a woman. I'm sure part of my decision was based on my feelings that the boys liked the quiet type more than the outgoing type, but I also remember a girl in my dorm at college who was quiet and sweet and smiled all the time, and it seemed everybody liked her. So, I figured if I were more like her, I'd be nicer, more likable and more successful.

So, as I sat on that bus all those hours, I determined that there was no reason I couldn't be just like the girl in my dorm. All I had to do was set my mind to it, and I could change my whole personality. Here was my perfect chance, and I was committed to doing just that.

I can still remember those first few days at the camp, as I concentrated so hard on being someone else. I had to think about it all the time and keep the picture of my dorm-mate in mind, so that I would remember to be like her. Mostly I just forced myself to be quiet and, instead of impressing people with how nice I was, they thought I was unfriendly. I really tried hard to be just like my friend at school, but let me tell you, I failed miserably. I could only keep it up a few short days, and the effect was not a good change in my personality, but rather it made me look and feel phony, which, of course, was true.

That was many years ago, and you'd think by now I would have gotten over this tendency to compare myself to others or try to be like someone else. However, it still crops up on occasion, and not long ago I found myself in that same spot again: comparing myself to someone else, trying to be what someone else wanted me to be. Even though I know better now, I still have to be on my guard against this bad habit, which I now recognize to be not only foolish, but also sinful.

Symptoms of this disease are an uneasiness in your spirit, feeling guilty about something but you're not quite sure what, knots in your stomach, discontent, and a general sense of gloom and despair. Can you recognize some of these things in yourself? Maybe it hits you only occasionally, or you may indeed find yourself continually consumed with comparing yourself to others and then not being satisfied with who you are.

David's Encouraging Example

There is a man in the Bible who knew that he had to be himself and not try to be someone else. I find his story a wonderful source of encouragement to me, and it helps to pull me out of that wrong thinking of comparing myself to others or trying to be like others. You'll find the story in 1 Samuel 17.

It's the story of David, the shepherd boy, who volunteered to go up against the giant, Goliath. Nobody else in the entire Israelite army had been willing to face this giant, even the experienced fighters. After all, Goliath was over nine feet tall and they were ordinary-sized men. They took one look at Goliath and the comparison convinced them it would be foolhardy to try to defeat such a large enemy.

The children of God were being held captive by this giant. Somebody had to defeat Goliath in order to have victory over their enemy, the Philistines, who would then be subjects of Israel and servants of Saul, the king.

David was on an errand to the fighting field, to take food to his brothers in the army, and he heard Goliath making his daily challenge, which he had been doing for forty days, every morning and evening. Actually, Goliath was mocking Israel, because he was certain nobody would ever fight him. So he was goading and taunting them.

When David heard Goliath's challenge, he wanted to know why they were allowing this bully to make these daily threats against the Lord's army. He couldn't understand why someone had not taken up Goliath's challenge. After all, the Lord was with the Israelite army!

His brother Eliab became very angry with David's questions, and basically told him to go back where he came from and tend the sheep. He belittled David and insulted him, telling him he was conceited and wicked, and he had only come to watch and comment on the battle. (No doubt Eliab was still struggling with the fact that David had been anointed by Samuel to become the next king instead of him!)

But David didn't let Eliab intimidate him. He kept asking questions, and finally King Saul heard about him and sent for him. David volunteered to go fight Goliath. Of course, Saul was reluctant to let him to do this, because David was only a boy and Goliath was a huge, experienced fighter. It would be folly to send David up against Goliath.

David insisted that he could face Goliath and related to Saul his experience in killing a lion and a bear. He said, "The Lord who delivered me from the paw of the lion and the paw of the bear will deliver me from the hand of this Philistine" (1 Sam. 17:37a).

So Saul relented; after all, nobody else was willing to even try, so he might as well let David have a go at it. Then Saul tried to tell David how to do it:

> Then Saul dressed David in his own tunic. He put a coat of armor on him and a bronze helmet on his head. David fastened on his sword over the tunic and tried walking around, because he was not used to them. "I cannot go in these," he said to Saul, "because I am not used to them." So he took them off. Then he took his staff in his hand, chose five smooth stones from the stream, put them in the pouch of his shepherd's bag and, with his sling in his hand, approached the Philistine. (1 Sam. 17:38-40)

You know the end of the story: David takes aim at Goliath's head, hits him in the right place, and with one stone he knocks him out. Then he cuts off Goliath's head with Goliath's own sword, and claims victory.

How did David defeat Goliath? By using his own slingshot. That's what he was good at; that's how he had defeated the lion and the bear; that's the gift God had given him and taught him how to use. If he had tried to defeat Goliath in Saul's armor, with a sword, he would never have won. David was smart enough to realize that he would make a huge mistake to try to do what God wanted him to do in someone else's armor.

David seems to have learned this important lesson at a very early age: Don't try to be like someone else. Don't compare yourself to others. Be who God has created you to be, using the gifts and experience God has given to you. Get over trying to wear someone else's "armor." Use your own slingshot!

It is very easy to look around and see other people who are successful and think: *That's what I should be doing.* Or *I should change who I am and be who she/he is.* God quietly teaches me again and again that I've been given certain gifts and others I have not been given. Instead of looking down on the gifts God has given to me and wishing I were like someone else, I should just use what I have and do it well. Yes, I can learn from others and certainly I can improve, but I can't be like anyone else.

Paul wrote to his young disciple Timothy: "For this reason I remind you to fan into flame the gift of God, which is in you through the laying on of my hands" (2 Tim. 1:6). Timothy didn't need to be like Paul or any of the other apostles. Timothy just needed to use his own slingshot, as it were, and take the gift God had invested in him to the next level—fan it into flame.

As I've struggled with comparing myself to others, this has become more and more my prayer, that God would help me to fan into flame the gift of God in me, rather than trying to be like someone else. I am learning to be content with who I am, even to thank God that I'm not like that wonderful young classmate whom I so much admired, but rather that I am created in God's image just the way I am and I don't need to be like others. As I've begun to appreciate God's creativity in me, it has freed me to appreciate others without envy or jealousy. It's no longer difficult to recommend other speakers or writers, people God uses in my own life to make me more like Jesus. I truly can admire their gifting and benefit from it without thinking about me or my gifting.

How I wish I had learned this lesson sooner in my life, but I can tell you that it has taken away so much unnecessary and sinful discontent with myself, and it has given me much greater freedom to fan into flame God's gifting in me.

Another important lesson in this David and Goliath story is that David was able to kill Goliath with a slingshot because, as a lowly shepherd boy, he had plenty of time to perfect his skill as a marksman. He had worked with that slingshot until he was an expert. And I'm sure he had time to sing and play a harp and write poetry and develop those incredible skills, too, while he was there, all by himself, in that seemingly unimportant, going-no-place job of taking care of dumb sheep!

I look back on my life and realize that in those quiet times of my life, when it looked like nothing was happening, even in times when I wasn't walking with the Lord, I was learning skills and doing things that have equipped me to do what God has me doing now. God is very efficient, and He knows how to prepare us for the job ahead. But we have to get over comparing ourselves to others and trying to be like others.

David had to be able to kill Goliath because that was the deed that would propel him to eventually become the king. It made his reputation and paved the way for God's plan for him. But it began in those lonely fields, shooting stones from a slingshot day in and day out, and learning how to kill big enemies in unconventional ways.

Of course, David didn't know when he was tending sheep that God was preparing him to be king. He had no idea. But he did that job well, and while he was doing it, he learned to do other things—like play a harp, write poetry, aim a slingshot really well, and tackle enemies that were much bigger than him. All these gifts were being developed to be used by God in the future.

Great athletes talk about "staying within themselves." That means they have to play the game using their strengths and not try to be like others. David knew how to "stay within himself" and not to mimic others or be intimidated when others told him what he should do or how he should do it.

The Sin of Comparing

Did you ever stop and think about what it really means when you compare yourself to others and try to be like someone else? It means you think God made a mistake in the way He made you. It means you would have created yourself differently if you'd had a choice. It demonstrates a lack of trust in God's wisdom; it says you think God was either wrong or cruel to make you the way you are.

Usually when we compare ourselves to others we come to one of three conclusions:

1. We're better than they are.

Think about the parable of the Pharisee and the tax collector, as given in Luke 18:9-14:

> To some who were confident of their own righteousness and looked down on everybody else, Jesus told this parable: "Two men went up to the temple to pray, one a Pharisee and the other a tax collector. The Pharisee stood up and prayed about himself: 'God, I thank you that I am not like other men—robbers, evildoers, adulterers—or even like this tax collector. I fast twice a week and give a tenth of all I get.' But the tax collector stood at a distance. He would not even look up to heaven, but beat his breast and said, 'God have mercy on me, a sinner.' I tell you that this man, rather than the other, went home justified before God."

We look at this Pharisee and think, "How awful!" And yet how easy it is for us to compare ourselves to others with that same type of attitude. Like the Pharisee, we compare outward appearances and end up thinking we're pretty hot stuff. That kind of comparison leads us into pride, and it causes us to form wrong conclusions about others.

How often do we form strong opinions based on how someone dresses, or how articulate they are, or how professional they seem. Admittedly I am prone to judge by outward appearances and jump to wrong conclusions. I can think of specific people in my life whom I wrongly judged because I looked at the outside instead of getting to know the real person. After getting to know them,

I had a totally different view, and almost always it went from negative to positive!

As the Lord said to Samuel when he was choosing the next king of Israel from among Jesse's sons (and he thought Eliab, the firstborn, would be God's choice), "Do not consider his appearance or his height, for I have rejected him. The Lord does not look at the things man looks at. Man looks at the outward appearance, but the Lord looks at the heart" (1 Sam. 16:7). The contrast between Eliab and David was evident in their interchange in the Valley of Elah, before David confronted Goliath. God saw Eliab's selfish, unbelieving heart, and even though he really looked the part of a king, he was not God's choice.

Do you find yourself looking at others and comparing them to yourself to their detriment? How often are you thinking: *Well, I look better than she does,* or *I perform better than he does,* or *I've got more to offer than they do?* I've found that I can sit in church and compare how I would do something to how someone else is doing it, thinking that my way would be better! When we make these kinds of comparisons, the sin of pride is taking over our minds. Jesus said at the end of this parable: "For everyone who exalts himself will be humbled, and he who humbles himself will be exalted" (Luke 18:14b).

Listen to yourself think and talk, and see how often you compare yourself to others and end up feeling pretty proud of yourself. It can happen so easily—believe me, I know! The apostle Paul wrote to the Philippians that they should consider others more important than themselves (Phil. 2:3). That's the attitude we need to have toward others.

What I find is particularly prevalent with people these days is that we compare our positions and our salaries, and think we're more important than others because we've climbed the ladder higher or gotten another raise. Certainly that's one of the real dangers we face if we are successful—the sin of pride in thinking that we're better than others because we've got a bigger title or office.

Remember that in eternity those titles and salaries will have no meaning. For a Christian they should simply be viewed as resources to be used by God. If you're in that very typical but sinful practice of comparing your status to others and judging worth based on position, please read carefully Philippians 2 and 1 Corinthians 4:6-7 and get over it!

2. They're better than we are.

Secondly, comparing ourselves to others can lead us to think that others are better than us. Consider the parable of the talents that Jesus gave us in Matthew 25:14-30. Before leaving on a long trip, the master gives three servants certain talents, or resources. One servant received five talents, one two, and the third servant received only one talent.

When the master returned, he asked each of them to give an account of what they had done with those resources. The first servant reported that his five talents were now ten; the second servant similarly reported that his two talents were now four. But what about the third servant? He had taken his one talent and done nothing with it, and he had to report to the master that because he was afraid of losing it, he had hidden it and it was still only one.

The master rewards the first two servants equally: "Well done, good and faithful servant! You have been faithful with a few things; I will put you in charge of many things. Come and share your master's happiness" (v. 21). Even though one had ten and one had only four, they got the exact same reward.

But what does the master say to the third servant? It's a very strong statement: "You wicked, lazy servant!...Take the talent from him and give it to the one who has ten talents," (vv. 26 and 28).

The lesson here is that God does not compare us with others, but He does expect us to make very good use of the resources that have been given to us. This servant could have had the same reward that the others received had he simply taken his one talent and used it. He wasn't required to multiply his one into ten, only into two. But instead he looked at his meager one talent, decided there wasn't much he could do with just one, no doubt felt that the talents had not been fairly distributed, and simply gave up.

Are you failing to use what God has given you? Do you compare yourself to others and conclude that they are better than you, they have more to work with than you do, they've got it easy, and you've got it hard? Whether you have more or less than other people is inconsequential in God's economy. You will be required to account for your own resources, no one else's.

Notice what happened to this third servant as a result of his attitude of comparing himself to those who had more:

- First, it made him fearful. He was afraid to lose the talent he had, since he compared and saw that he had only one. And that fear led him to a very irrational, unreasonable course of action. Knowing that the master was demanding and expected him to multiply his talents, he decided to dig a hole and hide it. Does that even make sense? No, but fear caused him to become irrational.

- Second, he became lazy. The master called him a lazy servant. When we compare ourselves to others who have more than we do, this will frequently happen. We lose our motivation, we lose our initiative; it becomes our excuse, and we shift the blame and become lazy.

- Third, it led him into sin. The master identified him as wicked, because he had failed to do what he knew he should do. In James 4:17, we read: "Anyone, then, who knows the good he ought to do and doesn't do it, sins."

- Fourth, he lost what he had. His worst fear was realized; the master took his one talent and gave it to the man with ten.

- Fifth, he lost his reward. Had he multiplied his one talent into two, had he been as good a steward of what he had as the others, even though the end result would have been only two talents, he would have received the same reward as the others, and would have been given more. But he lost his reward because he compared himself to those who had more, decided there was nothing much he could do with what he had, became fearful and lazy, and lost all he had.

3. *We envy them and feel that we've been cheated.*
Then, comparing ourselves to others can cause us to be envious and jealous. I think of the time when Peter fell into this trap after Jesus had risen and was about to ascend back to heaven. Jesus told Peter that He had plans to use

him mightily, but also informed him that he would be required to suffer for the Lord. His prophecy to Peter was: "'When you are old you will stretch out your hands, and someone else will dress you and lead you where you do not want to go.' Jesus said this to indicate the kind of death by which Peter would glorify God" (John 21:18b-19a).

Then Peter made the mistake of comparing himself to John. Peter asked Jesus, "Lord, what about John?" Jesus answered, "If I want him to remain alive until I return, what is that to you? You must follow me" (John 21:21b-22).

I think we can all empathize with Peter, because we've been there. When something bad happens to us, we tend to think, *Well, what about John (or whoever!)? Why should I have to endure all this? John's no better than me. Don't I deserve a break today, Lord? At least make everyone else suffer just like I'm suffering.*

What we have to recognize is that God is sovereign and He does as He pleases. It is His prerogative to lead each of us in whatever paths He chooses. When we start looking at others and thinking they've got it easy and we've got it hard, then we're in for trouble. That is envy, that is lack of trust, and that is sin.

Proverbs 14:30 says, "A heart at peace gives life to the body, but envy rots the bones." The sin of comparing ourselves to others almost always causes us to envy others, and that envy will backfire on you big time. Wise Solomon said it actually rots your bones—it affects your physical well-being in addition to affecting you spiritually. One of the attributes of real love, as described in 1 Corinthians 13, is that "It does not envy ..." (v. 4). So comparing ourselves to others is evidence of a lack of this kind of selfless love that we should have as disciples of Jesus Christ.

When I find myself falling into this pattern of thinking and comparing myself to others and wondering why I can't have things as easy as they do, I immediately try to remember what Jesus said to Peter, and I say to myself: *What is that to you, Mary? It's none of your business how God chooses to treat other people. Your job is simply to obey the Lord so that He will be glorified in your life.*

Appreciating Yourself

You are unique; there's no one else like you in the whole world. God is so infinitely creative, that He's able to give each of us unique traits and personalities, and He has designed you to be yourself. He has a purpose for you that no one else could exactly fulfill. He wants your personality, your type, to meet a certain need in the Kingdom of God.

Scripture tells us that we are fearfully and wonderfully made, that God knit us together in our mother's womb, that He is intimately acquainted with us down to counting the hairs on our heads, and we are each created in His image. Now, just put all those facts in your head, and consider what that means.

First of all, you're not a mistake. You've all heard little jokes like "When God was giving out brains, He forgot you." Or "When God was giving out looks, you thought He said books and you said, 'I don't want any.'" Well, maybe those jokes aren't as harmless as they seem, because they teach a basic untruth. God didn't make a mistake when He designed you. You were planned in the mind of God. It was not a haphazard coming together of atoms or molecules; you're not an accident of nature. You are designed according to God's plan.

Secondly, what you are is like what God is. You are created in the image of God. Now, don't confuse this with New Age teaching that says we're all gods. That certainly is not true. But it is true that we are all created in God's image. That means my personality traits are like God's. Part of God's personality is just like my personality, because I'm created in His image. I'm outgoing, assertive, entrepreneurial, energetic, and so is God, for I'm created in His image.

It is very important that you understand this basic truth of Scripture. It will change your whole attitude toward who you are. I remember when it first began to dawn on me that God had given me this personality for a purpose. It was long after my experience at the Christian summer camp. I left there thinking I was stuck with who I was, still wishing I could be different, but disheartened to realize I had to settle for who I was, because I couldn't change my personality.

I thought that my personality would have been much more acceptable for a man. Being an assertive woman didn't fit in with my idea of what a Christian woman should be. So, I was confused for quite a while as to why I had this personality. Then I began to learn that God had not made a mistake, He did not forget that I was a female when He designed me, and He had a purpose for designing me, a woman, the way I am.

As I've become more and more comfortable with who I am and the way I've been created, then I've learned to enjoy and appreciate who I am. You know, I don't think I'd really want to be anyone else any longer. I like the way God created me.

Now, it's okay to say that. It's okay for you to say that about yourself. Go ahead, say it: *I like the way God created me*. All you're doing is affirming that God doesn't make mistakes, and you are pleased with His creation. That's not pride, assuming your heart attitude is correct. That is simply thanking God for His creativity in you and recognizing that His creation is good.

God wants you to be pleased with the way He has created you, for it shows that you trust Him. It shows that you believe His Word is true and that the way you are created is the best, since it is God's creation. I'm not talking about thinking you're better than anyone else. Absolutely not. But we can appreciate who we are as God's unique creation, while also appreciating His creativity in others.

Learning to accept who we are doesn't mean we give up on trying to improve. While it's true God has given me a certain type of personality, it's also true that my personality has a lot of rough edges which need polishing. We have to understand that sin has affected God's perfect creation, and so until we get to heaven, our personalities are damaged by the sin factor. So, while learning to accept that I am created especially by God just the way I am, I also know that I'm never all I can be, and I must continually allow God to file down the rough edges in me, the things about my personality which are not Christ-like.

We read in Genesis 1 that God looked at what He had created and six times He said, "It is good." He created you the way you are, and He looked at you and said, "It is good." Can you not, then, trust your loving Creator and believe that the way He created you is good?

When you truly believe that, it makes such a difference in your life. It frees you up to be who you are. As long as we don't like the way we're created, as long as we're wishing or trying to be like others, then obviously we can't achieve what God has intended us to do. It ties you up in knots; it's like facing life with both hands tied behind your back.

When you don't like who you are, you become something you are not, which is phony, uncomfortable, and ineffective, and you never realize the wonderful potential of what God created you to be. But as soon as you can accept yourself and believe that God has made you for special and unique purposes, then you're free. Now the person God has created starts to shine through beautifully; now you begin to see just why God made you the way you are; now you discover that there was a lot there you didn't even recognize before. God is free to work in and through you when you're free to say, "Thank You, Jesus, You didn't make a mistake when You made me. Now please take what You have made and polish it and refine it, and use it for the purposes You intended."

If you are in the bad habit of frequently comparing yourself to others, I strongly encourage you to get over it! It is wrong thinking, and that will lead you to think you're better than others, or others are better than you, or it will lead you into envy. All of those things are wrong and sinful. By God's grace we can get over this very harmful practice of comparing ourselves, and learn to be thankful for who we are and how God has blessed us, multiplying the resources He has given us to bring glory to His name.

Chapter Three

Get Over
Needing the
Approval of Others

I've often said, "I may not be good, but I'm fast!" I am able somehow to keep many balls in the air and be pretty productive, getting lots done in short amounts of time. And I'm quite serious when I say that my speed often cripples the quality of my work. Nonetheless, I seem to get lots done, and I used to feed off the approval that I would get from others as a result. "I don't know how you do all you do!" "You are so busy; how do you do it all?" "You amaze me. How did you do that?" These were the kind of comments that came my way pretty regularly and, without realizing it, I developed an approval addiction.

I thrived on this approval; it was a huge part of my motivation and my sense of well-being. It was true in my career in sales and marketing, and it was—and sadly sometimes still is—true in my ministry. As I grew in my knowledge of God and became a bit more spiritually mature, this need for approval became more apparent to me. And because I needed others to tell me that I was doing well—that I was doing better than others—that I was part superwoman, I was not open to constructive criticism. I chafed at any suggestion that what I did was lacking in some way.

I remember early on in my ministry I had spoken at a morning session at a church and was taking a brief break before the afternoon session. Someone then delivered a note to me from one of the women; she was making a suggestion that a certain way I was presenting something was not effective and I should consider doing it differently—or not doing it at all. I can still recall the immediate reaction I had as I read her note: *How dare she criticize me? Did she think she could do a better job than I was doing? It wasn't as easy as it looked.* I withered under any criticism of my performance because I so desperately needed approval from others.

That's one sign of an approval addiction—you resent and reject criticism or even gentle suggestions. Another sign is that you try to solicit approval from others. Some of us can do that rather subtly so that it doesn't come across as bragging or begging, but secretly we are trying to get someone to affirm what we've done or who we are.

It took a while for me to recognize and come to grips with my approval addiction, but I remember when I began to realize that I was being recognized and remembered for being busy and productive. I started to ask myself, *Is that how you really want to be remembered? Do you want your tombstone to read, "Here lies a very busy woman"?* After acknowledging my approval addiction and praying about it, I honestly have come to the place where I almost recoil inwardly when anyone gives me that kind of affirmation. I'm still busy and I don't know that I'll ever slow down a great deal. It's who I am and how God has created me, but the need for others to approve of my abilities to perform has pretty much been replaced by a much better approval addiction—and that is to stand before Jesus at the Judgment Seat for believers and hear Him say, "Well done, good and faithful servant."

Why do we need the approval of others?
Quite honestly, I think we're all born with the need for approval and we seek it from our earliest years. Little two-year-olds catch on that they get approval by doing something cute. We teach our children to perform, and in the performing of the song or the dance or dunking a basketball—or whatever—our children learn that performance brings approval. My daughter walked at a very early age, like seven months, and I paraded her in front of anyone who would watch so that they would approve of my very advanced daughter! (No doubt I was needing approval as the mother of a very gifted child!)

We all need approval, but how do we become addicted to this need? It often begins in our early years. If your parents withheld approval from you, if they were more focused on punishment and correction than affirmation and approval, this could be a major cause of your approval addiction. If you never received recognition from other authority figures in your life—such as teachers or bosses— even late in life you could have developed an inordinate need for approval. If you are very competitive by nature, as I am, and you have to win, to be number one, in order to feel approved, this could be part of the cause for your need for approval.

It's always helpful to understand the source of our struggles, but using them as excuses does nothing but keep us powerless, in bondage to them. We're adults now; it's time to get over it and live free from needing other people to validate us.

After a ten-year spiritual detour in my life, when I wandered far from God in my desperate search to find the right man to marry me, as I began to make Jesus lord of my life, gradually He revealed areas in my life that needed healing, areas where I needed to "get over it" and move on. I remember when I finally realized that my deep desire to have a man in my life was in large part because I needed the approval and acceptance that would come with the right man on my arm.

I wanted people to say, "Wow, she must be really special because look who she's with!" I needed to be validated by having others say I was okay—indeed, I was outstanding—because I had attracted and landed an outstanding man. When I first saw this in my heart, I was just overwhelmed at how insecure I was and how this kind of thinking was a recipe for disaster. For years I was obsessed and imprisoned by this need, and I never really saw it for what it was until many years later.

How do we get over our need for the approval of others?

Here's what I think: We don't! It's a basic need that's born in us. Some of us have a greater approval need than others, but we all need approval in order to survive, to thrive, to be motivated and affirmed. What we have to do is to look for approval in the right place! Instead of asking other people to meet our need, and finding that it is never completely satisfactory or never quite enough, we need to live our lives for the approval of our Savior, Jesus Christ.

This requires us to have a clear assurance of our personal relationship with the living God. And that begins when we become His child through faith in Jesus Christ. Once that is firmly established, then we become more and more confident of God's approval and of our assurance in how He sees us as we delve into the Word of God, learn it, love it, study it, teach it, read it, memorize it, and obey it. If you wanted a quick fix, sorry, I don't have one because there aren't any. Jesus said, "Now this is eternal life: that they may know you, the only true God, and Jesus Christ, whom you have sent" (John 17:3). All that we need for life—including approval—is ours through the pursuit of knowing God and His Son, Jesus. It is a by-product of seeking first the kingdom of God and His righteousness.

So how much of your life is devoted to getting to know God? Is it simply one hour on Sunday mornings, or a two-hour Bible study every other week with a small group? That's good, but it's not enough. Knowing God and Jesus takes time, just as it takes time to know anyone. But unlike pursuing the knowledge of people, where usually the more you know the more you are disappointed (and vice versa), getting to know God is increasingly amazing and satisfying.

My ten-year hiatus from my relationship with God took me into a desperate approval addiction, which became a downward spiral into disappointment and discontentment. After I relinquished the control of my life to God and began a serious pursuit of getting to know Him, devoting significant time and effort immersed in His Word, serving Him, etc., I woke up one day to the realization that my approval addiction was fading. I wasn't trying to get over my need for the approval of others; instead I was developing a growing desire to please the Lord, and in the process I cared less and less whether people approved of me or not.

The apostle Paul tells us how to do this:

> So we make it our goal to please him (the Lord), whether we are at home in the body or away from it. (2 Cor. 5:9)

> Am I now trying to win the approval of men, or of God? Or am I trying to please men? If I were still trying to please men, I would not be a servant of Christ. (Gal. 1:10)

> We are not trying to please men but God, who tests our hearts ... We were not looking for praise from men, not from you or anyone else. (1 Thess. 2:4, 6)

> We instructed you how to live in order to please God, as in fact you are living. Now we ask you and urge you in the Lord Jesus to do this more and more. (1 Thess. 4:1)

Our need for approval has to have a complete makeover. We have to consciously make it our goal to please the Lord and stop trying to please people. That means we have to renew our minds, clean out the old addictions for the approval of people and replace them with a consuming desire to please the Lord.

Notice in Galatians Paul says he is not still trying to please men, which means he had tried to at some point in his life. He switched his need for approval from people to God. That's our assignment, too. Now, what does that look like in our everyday lives?

It begins with prayer. Choose one or two of the verses above and pray it into your life each morning. For example, your prayer might be:

> Lord, today it is my goal to please You. I want Your
> approval today. I want to live in such a way today that
> You will be pleased and You will approve. I can only do
> this through Your power in me. So I pray that my mind
> and my emotions will be under Your control.

Praying directly from Scripture is the most powerful way
to pray, and you can be assured that when you pray based
on God's Word, you are praying like you should and God
is honored. It will please Him—He will approve!

Then, identify the people in your life whose approval
you have desired, but who have never satisfied your need
for approval. That could go way back to your parents,
other family members, teachers, bosses, mates, children ...
whoever. It will be helpful if you will name those people to
God and to yourself. Pray specifically that God will show
you whose approval you have been addicted to, and why
you needed their approval so much.

There may have been people in your life who should have
given you approval and affirmation, but they didn't. But
blaming them or holding a grudge against them will never
set you free from your need for their approval. As long as
you keep trying to win their approval, or you hold bitterness
in your heart because it was never given, they will continue
to have power over you. You are giving them that power
because you haven't let go of your need for their approval.

God can empower you to get over your approval
addictions, no matter how deeply imbedded they are in
your mind, and no matter how much you deserve approval.

A Personal Story
My friend Carol tells of her battle with approval addiction
and how God is delivering her:

My upbringing was in a normal home for those of us who can relate to being raised in the fifties and sixties. Dad was the provider and protector, while mom was the homemaker.

Thankfully, my mother's love was unconditional, whereas my father's was somewhat performance-based. Out of deep love and respect, I did not want to displease him. Then too, my older sister was a hard act to follow as everyone expected me to be exactly like her when, in fact, we are polar opposites in many ways. For years I felt I had to measure up and struggled with my perceived shortcomings. Perfectionism and an inferiority complex left me with low self-esteem.

I used to be a people-pleaser and would do whatever it took to be liked. My first mistake was marrying someone of whom my father disapproved. I hate to say my father was right but within two years I was divorced. This precipitated an even worse decision when I chose a convicted felon for my second husband. I thought no self-respecting man would want a divorcee but someone with the stigma of prison would certainly approve of and not judge *my* status. Twenty-two years later, that too ended in another divorce with worse consequences of immoral living and an addiction for which I blamed my spouse. At fifty years of age, I finally took responsibility for my own life and choices.

When I came to understand grace, when I came to appreciate God's approval because I stand forgiven having accepted Jesus Christ as my Savior, when I comprehended His death on the cross as the atonement for my sin—the striving ceased.

Carol says it's okay to look back, but don't park there. That's a really good piece of advice. She has looked back enough to understand her approval addiction, but no longer does she blame her father or her ex-husbands, no longer does she harbor a root of bitterness toward them. Jesus has renovated her life and cleansed her mind, and she has a "future and a hope" because of Him.

Living Free from Needing the Approval of Others

Just think about the difference it would make in your life if you were truly striving for God's approval instead of the approval of people. First, you would be free from that driving need to be recognized by others. If we are truly seeking God's approval, then earthly approval will become less and less important to us.

When you're working for the Lord's approval, you're free from being a slave to people. You no longer have to jump through hoops or compromise your standards or spend money or waste time trying to get someone to notice you. You don't have to try to be a super-person in order to impress people.

In his book, *The Relationship Principles of Jesus* (a book I highly recommend), Tom Holladay writes:

> Imagine for just a moment the incredible freedom of humility—being set free from the need to be noticed, from worrying about which seat you are sitting in or not sitting in. Being set free to trust God and to live out his ambition for your life. Real freedom![1]

And in speaking further of humility, Tom says:

> Don't try to feel humble—it's spiritual quicksand; just act humble.[2]

---

1   *The Relationship Principles of Jesus*, p. 293, Zondervan, Grand Rapids, MI ©2008.

2   *Ibid*, p. 292.

This is some of the best advice you'll ever receive, and it works on so many different levels. We are so prone to let our feelings govern our actions, and our feelings can be so distorted, abused, confused, and/or warped that they take us down the wrong paths. Learning to acknowledge your feelings and admit them but refuse to let them control you is a sign of maturity—emotional and spiritual maturity. Feelings must be addressed and many times they are symptoms that something in our spirits needs healing. So they are not to be ignored, and, of course, when they are positive they add great joy to our lives. But they must be in subjection to our minds, and our minds must be controlled by the mind of Christ, which is in us when we are born from above (1 Cor. 2:16).

So, let me paraphrase Tom's advice about humility for our purposes here:

> Don't try to stop pleasing people—it's impossible to do; just start trying to please God.

That is replacing wrong thinking with right thinking, which is a principle I explain in detail in my book, *Think About What You Think About*. Truly it is a simple principle: In order to change our behavior, we have to first change our thinking. And the only way to get rid of wrong thinking is to replace it with right thinking.

Become a Dispenser of Approval

As we learn to get over our addictive need for the approval of others, it should cause us to become more sensitive to how others need our approval. In a recent conversation with a dear friend, she suggested that a congratulatory note from me to her granddaughter would be so encouraging to her because she values my opinion and approval. This was a total surprise to me because I never even thought that her granddaughter cared whether I approved or not. We have limited contact because of distance and our lives don't touch very often. But if my approval in a simple note can encourage her, why not?

As parents we have a special responsibility to give our children approval when and where appropriate. Of course, they must be taught and corrected and punished at times, but there should be many more doses of approval than of correction. A child who grows up knowing she or he is approved by his/her parents is going to avoid lots of the pitfalls of approval addiction. My father was extreme and definitely immodest in his approval of his children, grandchildren and great-grandchildren. He simply thought we were all the best and he didn't hesitate to express his opinion! Early in my career when I worked for IBM, he would say, "Mary could be President of IBM if she wanted to," and there was no way I could dissuade him of his fallacious and ridiculous opinion. As embarrassing as that was at times, I was so blessed to have a father who approved of me and expressed his approval freely.

We can become God's touch to others – His voice through our voice, our notes, our phone calls, our emails – that lets someone know God cares about them. I have a long way to go but I'm determined to become a better dispenser of approval to others when it is deserved. They may not need it, but it's a way to encourage others and a way to focus on the needs of others, rather than my own needs.

If the need for the approval of others has held far too much control over you, and if you recognize your need to get over it, I pray you will let God set you free. It is a bondage that keeps you from the "joy of your salvation" and the freedom that Christ died to give you.

Chapter Four

Get Over
Wrong Attitudes

"**A**ttitudes are contagious. Would anyone want to catch yours?" Somewhere years ago I heard that cliché but I didn't give attitudes much thought for a long time. However, in my years of teaching customer-service skills, I realized that the most important attribute and skill for a good customer-service rep was a person's attitude. And you can't teach it! There is no formula for it, no twelve-step program to guarantee you will have a good, positive attitude. It is something each of us must do for ourselves or it simply won't happen.

It is reported that Bill Marriott, the founder of Marriott Hotels, said, "I don't hire people and ask them to be nice; I hire nice people." Obviously, he recognized that the right attitude is the basic requirement for a good employee. Most other skills and abilities can be taught, but attitudes are internal thermometers that we develop, nurture, and maintain, and we are in control of our attitudes, good or bad.

In an age when shifting blame has become an accepted explanation for almost anything, we can look at our wrong attitudes and find a scapegoat, a person to blame.

- *You wouldn't be positive if you worked for my boss.*

- *I'd be happy if I weren't married to her.*

- *Well, what do you expect—my children are driving me crazy!*

- *How can I look on the bright side when I have just got laid off?*

The simple truth is no one or nothing can cause you to have a bad attitude if you decide not to have one; and conversely, no one or nothing can make you have a good attitude if you choose to remain negative. In talking recently with a wonderful young couple in our church, I learned—almost coincidentally—that he had just been fired from a job he had held for fourteen years since graduating from college. It was a sudden turn of events caused by his decision to express his opinion to his manager and make a suggestion for improving the company. And just like that—overnight—he was given his marching orders.

I know this man well enough to know that whatever he said or did was done in the right spirit and for good reasons. In fact, this man is the youngest elder ever elected in our church, which is a testimony to his character and Christian integrity. In telling me this, he said that he had been unhappy with some of the company's decisions for a while, and he and his wife had been praying that God would give direction as to whether he should look for another job or not. So they laughed and said that God had answered their prayers. There was not one tinge of bitterness or blame. He did not malign any person in the company or shift the blame in any way. He simply believes this was God's answer to his prayer, and that it is time for him to move on.

In this economy, finding a new job at his experience level will not be easy. But his attitude and that of his supportive wife as well were simply amazing. No doubt they had some anxious moments at first, but they have gotten over it and are moving on to the new thing that God has for them.

What is an attitude anyway?

My online dictionary says it is "A settled way of thinking or feeling, typically reflected in a person's behavior." Another one says it is "An organized predisposition to respond in a favorable or unfavorable manner toward a specified class of objects."

We all have attitudes toward life, toward certain people and circumstances, toward work and health and truth —to name a few—and these have been shaped by our personalities, our life experiences, our education, and by many people who have influenced our attitudes. We are predisposed to respond in positive or negative ways based on our attitudes. Our behavior reflects our attitudes—and that includes the words we speak, the looks on our faces, our body language, how we spend our time and money— ad infinitum. Our attitudes have a profound effect on every area of our lives.

Yet I dare say that many Christians—and people in general—are like the way I was: totally oblivious to their own attitudes, rarely, if ever, thinking about the condition or state of them. I'm convinced most of us see ourselves as having positive attitudes in general because we've just never taken a measure of our own attitudes.

In order to help us get over some wrong attitudes that are keeping us mired down, I want to encourage you to evaluate your own attitude in the following specific areas. The truth is we can have good attitudes in some areas and not-so-good ones in others. No doubt you'll be able to relate to some of these.

Your General Attitude

Generally when we talk about attitudes, we are addressing whether we have a positive or negative attitude toward life. Whether we see the glass as half empty or half full. Whether we look on the bright side or the dark side. Whether we imagine the best or the worst.

Have you ever known people who were almost always negative? If you say they look nice, they tell you how terrible their hair is. If you say the weather is lovely, they insist it will rain tomorrow. If you compliment someone's performance, they tell you how it doesn't measure up. You know when you see them coming that they will have something negative to say about something or someone. They truly see every glass as half empty.

Then there is the eternally positive person. Every glass is half full; every person is nice; every day is a good day. Smiles are abundant and encouragement is their language.

Admittedly, most of us are somewhere in between those two extremes. The questions we need to ask ourselves are:

- Do I ever really think about my attitude in general?

- Would most people describe me as a generally positive person or not?

- In any given day, how often do I reflect on whether I'm responding positively or negatively?

- How would I describe my own general attitude?

Here are some things you can do to measure your attitude in general and make corrections if needed:

- Choose a day when you determine you will say nothing negative for the entire day. Make a commitment to pay attention all day long to everything you say and think, and focus on keeping everything positive. You may discover, as I did, that your speech was far more negative than you ever thought it was.

- Ask a close friend/mate/relative/co-worker to give you some kind of simple signal when you start into negative territory. It could be a reciprocal accountability exercise for both of you. Accountability is a good tool to help us change behavior.

- Determine that you will say something nice to everyone you interact with in your day—family, friends, co-workers, clerks, strangers—everybody. If that pushes you out of your comfort zone, it might indicate that you just don't do it often enough.

- Make certain that the first words you speak each morning—out loud or to yourself—are encouraging words. Start your day in positive territory.

- Walk away from griping sessions or conversations, if possible, or at least refuse to contribute to them.

With a little focus on your attitude, and some intentional steps to make you a more positive, upbeat person, you could see pretty dramatic improvement in your stress levels, your energy levels, your productivity—and yes, in your relationships. It's worth a try.

Your Attitude toward Your Lot in Life

People who continually see themselves as disadvantaged, as having been given a "raw deal," as victims of people or circumstances, have allowed themselves to develop a very destructive attitude. This is not to say that some people seem to have much more difficult situations in life than others; that is obvious. And many times it is puzzling. Life is not fair and it's one of the hardest things for us to accept. But allowing yourself to wallow in the unfairness or inequity of your life's situation is a recipe for unhappiness.

I remember my niece telling me that they did not allow their four children to use the word "fair." It was a forbidden four-letter word in their home when the children were growing up. I'm sure you've noticed that children are very prone to use the "it's not fair" argument when trying to get what they want. My niece and her husband were trying to teach their children that life is not fair, and you have to deal with it. Don't expect everybody to treat you fairly; don't look for perfect justice in life. It's not going to happen. It's wise for parents to teach their children from early ages this fact, because the sooner they understand it, the better prepared they will be to deal with the unfairness of life.

Caution is needed here because understanding that life is not fair could in itself be a negative attitude. The point is that if we put ourselves in the "life has not been fair to me" category, if that is how we think about ourselves, if we frequently talk about how we never get a break or how people always take advantage of us, then we are allowing this victim attitude to control our lives.

Your Attitude toward Work

Remember in Snow White and the Seven Dwarfs how the dwarfs marched off singing, "Hi-ho, hi-ho, it's off to work we go!" They were carrying those shovels and pickaxes into the mines singing with joyful voices and faces as though they couldn't wait to get to work.

Is that how you head off each day when you go to work? For you is it, "Hi-ho, hi-ho!"? Or is it, "I owe, I owe! So, it's off to work I go!"? Or maybe it's "Oh no, Oh, no, it's off to work I go." Is your job simply a necessary drudgery in your life? Instead of the ever-popular "Thank God It's Friday!", can you ever really be thankful for a new working week? Do you ever approach Mondays with a thankful attitude?

Most people have the attitude that work is something they have to do in order to acquire all the things they want or need. Work is more often seen as a curse rather than a blessing. That's really sad because work and working environments were ordained by God, blessed by God, and ordered by God. In short, we were created to work, and that's where we get our dignity as humans.

God intended that our work would be a part of our identity, and that's the way it was originally. But once sin entered the picture through the disobedience of Adam and Eve, everything good that God created was corrupted, including work. The Garden of Eden, the first workplace created by God, was corrupted by sin, and your workplace has been corrupted by sin.

You'll find that curse in Genesis 3 where God said to Adam:

> Cursed is the ground because of you; through painful toil you will eat of it all the days of your life. It will produce thorns and thistles for you, and you will eat the plants of the field. By the sweat of your brow you will eat your food until you return to the ground (17b-19a).

Paraphrase: *You'll have to work, like you've been doing, but now work is going to be full of difficulties. You'll earn your living, but the thorns and thistles will make it unpleasant and it will be painfully toilsome at times. Your work will be hard and make you weary and tired.*

A secular writer, Studs Terkel, wrote a best-seller entitled *Working,* and here is his description of work:

> This book, being about work, is, by its very nature, about violence—to the spirit as well as to the body. It is about ulcers as well as accidents, about shouting matches as well as fistfights, about nervous breakdowns as well as kicking the dog around. It is, above all (or beneath all), about daily humiliations. To survive the day is triumph enough for the walking wounded among the great many of us.[1]

Wow! You can't blame us for not wanting to work in this cursed environment. If only we didn't have to earn a living! If only we could be spared this unpleasant and unfair predicament called work!! Isn't that the way we often think? We just hold our collective breath and live for the days we don't have to go to those corrupted workplaces! *Thank God it's Friday! My vacation is next week!! I'm retiring in two years!!! Let me out of here!!!!*

---

1   *Working,* by Studs Terkel, page xi, The New Press, New York, 1974.

But here's the really great news, from Galatians 3:13:

Christ redeemed us from the curse of the law by becoming a curse for us, for it is written: "Cursed is everyone who is hung on a tree."

Jesus Christ came to redeem us from the whole curse, including the curse on work. I don't think many Christians have ever understood that work was cursed, or that they have been set free from that curse. We seem to know that we've been set free from the curse of condemnation; our sins are forgiven; we will spend eternity in heaven with Jesus. But we've also been set free from the curse that was placed on work.

Here are two suggestions to help you get over any wrong attitude you may have acquired toward work in general or toward the specific job you now have.

• Work for the Lord, not for people.

Whatever you do, work at it with all your heart, as working for the Lord, not for men. (Col. 3:23)

Change employers. Before you begin your job each day, repeat out loud something like this:

Today I work for Jesus. I will be accountable to Him for my performance, my attitude, and my relationships with those I work with and for. Therefore, I will keep this thought in my mind all day long and, regardless of what is going on around me, I will work for the Lord today and seek to earn His approval.

Put Colossians 3:23 on your screen saver. Type it on a card and stick in on your desk or someplace where you can see it all day.

• **Do your work well.**

> Whatever your hand finds to do, do it with all your might ... (Eccles. 9:10)

Perform the duties of your job with excellence, thoroughness, dependability, accuracy, and extra-mile effort. Remember, you are working for the Lord, not man, and He will reward your good work effort. Besides, He deserves the best.

Your Prejudicial Attitudes

In our "enlightened" age, most of us think we have moved beyond being prejudiced against someone simply because they are a different nationality or race. But some of these attitudes have been so deeply imbedded in our minds that we need to take another look and see if we need to get over some prejudicial attitudes that we may harbor toward other races.

I am a middle-class, white woman and I'm certain there are prejudices within me that I don't even recognize. Furthermore, though I may think I understand racial prejudice and never participate in it myself, because I am a white woman, I'll never be able to totally understand what it feels like to be treated prejudicially simply because my skin is not white.

But as a Christian woman, I have a strong obligation to work hard at rooting out any prejudices I may have toward other races, and in extending myself to understand and relate to the people of other races, particularly my sisters and brothers in Christ.

The apostle Peter had to learn about racial prejudice. In Acts 10, we read the story of Cornelius, an Italian, who wanted to know the true God, the God of Israel, and

Peter was commanded in a vision to share the truth about Jesus with him and his family. Peter didn't want to do that because he was prejudiced toward all other races. He believed the gospel was only for the Jews, and he felt these other races were inferior and unworthy of God's grace. But in this vision he saw all kinds of animals and reptiles and birds, and a voice told him to kill and eat them. Peter refused because they were impure and unclean, but in the vision God said to him, "Do not call anything impure that God has made clean."

So, Peter shared the gospel with Cornelius and later he said, "I now realize how true it is that God does not show favoritism but accepts men from every nation who fear him and do what is right" (Acts 10:34-35). Peter began to face the prejudice that was within him and to realize how wrong it was. God has created all of the races and never once does He declare one to be better or more important than the other. Quite the opposite.

Jesus taught through His example that He was never racially prejudiced. Think of His encounter with the Samaritan woman. The Jews never spoke to Samaritans. They considered them second-class citizens; they would avoid them at all costs. But Jesus not only initiated a conversation with a Samaritan woman, He chose to reveal to her some incredible truth about Himself.

Years ago I was doing some training at a large hospital in downtown Detroit, and most of the people in my classes were African-Americans. At one point they began to share with me some of the racial abuse they had suffered from people calling the hospital. One woman told me about a man who asked her, "Are you black?" "Yes, I am," she replied. "Well, I'm a German," he said, "and we Germans hate blacks. You should have never been born." And with that, he hung up on her. (Be assured that his statement was blatantly wrong: Not all Germans hate blacks. In fact, I'm sure very few do. But that attitude had been passed on to him, no doubt, by parents and some very bad influences in his life. And that same attitude could be attributed to others who have been taught to hate other races.)

As she told me this, I could see and feel the pain of those inhumane, evil comments, and as the group talked about their experiences, I could feel the bitterness and anger inside of them. And I could certainly understand it.

Thinking about it later, I wondered, "How will we ever solve this problem of racial prejudice?" It's obvious that legislation can't change people's hearts, and when people are taught hate and prejudice by their parents, how in the world are we going to change those people?

As followers of Jesus Christ, we know that in Him we are one and, because of Jesus, these racial prejudices and attitudes can be erased from our minds. Jesus Christ is the unifying person who can bring us together and cure this horrible evil of racial prejudice. The sad news is, however, that even within the Body of Christ we find some of these prejudicial attitudes. It is a disgrace to the saving power of Jesus Christ for those of us who are born from above to continue to harbor racial prejudice of any kind. It's wrong; it's a sin. We must confront it in ourselves and in our communities, and let others know that it is intolerable within the Body of Christ.

How can we do that? Through friendships, through prayer. How many friends do you have of another race than your own? If we're ever going to get past our racial prejudices, we've got to get to know each other better and understand this prejudice through the eyes of our friends. One of the great joys of my ministry for me is that we have a strong balance of races at our seminars, luncheons, retreats, and in the Sunday class I teach. It's very colorful, and that's the way I like it.

I've formed some strong friendships with women of other races over the years, and you know, I rarely ever think about the color of their skin. But when I think about prejudice in our society toward them, I hurt for them. I feel it in a way I never would if they were not my friends. I see prejudice in our society much more realistically because I have some friends whom I love who happen to have a different skin color than mine.

Can't you see how this kind of racial prejudice is a weapon used very effectively by our enemy, Satan? He has managed to divide us and cause so much pain and hurt, even within the Body of Christ, based on racial prejudice. When we are one in Christ, there is no color differentiation. Paul wrote to the Galatians: "You are all sons of God through faith in Christ Jesus, for all of you who were baptized into Christ have clothed yourselves with Christ. There is neither Jew nor Greek, slave nor free, male nor female, for you are all one in Christ Jesus" (Gal. 3:26-28).

Other prejudices that are more subtle, and therefore more difficult to recognize, are our prejudicial attitudes toward people in different economical situations. In Job 34:19, we are reminded that God "shows no partiality to princes and does not favor the rich over the poor, for they are all the work of his hands ..." James puts it even more graphically. He writes: "Suppose a man comes into your meeting wearing a gold ring and fine clothes, and a poor man in shabby clothes also comes in. If you show special attention to the man wearing fine clothes and say, 'Here's a good seat for you,' but say to the poor man, 'You stand there' or 'Sit on the floor by my feet,' have you not discriminated among yourselves and become judges with evil thoughts?" (James 2:2-4)

We all tend to judge people by the way they're dressed, by their accumulation of wealth or things, by the way they walk or carry themselves. An interesting experiment is to notice how you're treated when you go shopping dressed professionally, versus shopping with your casual jeans or sweats on. Try it sometime; you'll see how the clerks in the stores are just naturally prejudiced against the sloppy look but give much more attention to you when you're well dressed. It's a tendency we all have.

James goes on to say in verse 5: "Has not God chosen those who are poor in the eyes of the world to be rich in faith and to inherit the kingdom he promised those who love him?" Have you noticed that it's much easier for a poor person to be committed to Jesus Christ than it is for a rich one? Jesus tried to tell His disciples that when He said it's easier for a camel to go through the eye of a needle than for a rich man to enter the kingdom of heaven. When the disciples heard that, they were greatly astonished and asked, "Who then can be saved?" (Matt. 19:24-25).

You see, the disciples were really focused on a person's financial status. Probably even more than in our day, the wealthy person was given homage, and they were astonished to hear Jesus say that it was hard for a rich person to enter the kingdom of heaven. Of course, Jesus went on to say it is possible with God because all things are possible with God.

But people very close to God are often very much without the world's measure of success—money and economical status. That meek person—the one who looks pitiful, doesn't know how to dress, and perhaps doesn't wear the best perfume—they are just as important to God as anyone else. And they may indeed know God better than those who are rich. Not because they're poor, but because their money doesn't get in their way.

Are you harboring some attitudes toward other people that are prejudicial? Isn't it time to get over it? It's wrong, it's sinful, and it's keeping you from God's best for you.

Our Challenge

In thinking of our attitudes, here are some passages that should speak directly to us.

> May the God who gives endurance and encouragement give you the same attitude of mind toward each other that Christ Jesus had, so that with one mind and one voice you may glorify the God and Father of our Lord Jesus Christ. (Rom. 15:5-6)

> You were taught, with regard to your former way of life, to put off your old self, which is being corrupted by its deceitful desires; to be made new in the attitude of your minds; and to put on the new self, created to be like God in true righteousness and holiness. (Eph. 4:22-24)

> For the word of God is alive and active. Sharper than any double-edged sword, it penetrates even to dividing soul and spirit, joints and marrow; it judges the thoughts and attitudes of the heart.(Heb. 4:12)

> Your attitude should be the same as that of Christ Jesus: Who, being in very nature God, did not consider equality

with God something to be grasped, but made himself nothing, taking the very nature of a servant, being made in human likeness. And being found in appearance as a man, he humbled himself and became obedient to death— even death on a cross! (Phil. 2:5-8)

These passages teach us important principles about our attitudes:

- We need to develop an attitude like Jesus had. That comes through prayer and knowing God's Word.

- Our attitudes are formed in our minds, in our thoughts, and therefore our minds need to be cleansed from wrong attitudes. We must learn to detect wrong thinking and replace it with biblical thinking.

- The Word of God is the tool God uses to help us get over wrong attitudes. The more you know it, the more you'll get over wrong attitudes.

- To have an attitude like Jesus, we must have a servant attitude. That means seeing ourselves as servants to others.

It's a tall assignment. You won't get there on your own. But if you will become intentional about changing your wrong attitudes, if you will pray and ask God to empower you to get over them, I promise you that you can do it—through Christ who gives you strength. And in the process, your joy will be greatly enhanced, your stress will be greatly reduced, and your relationships, your work, your productivity, and your effectiveness will be greatly improved. Based on the authority of God's Word, I guarantee it!

Chapter Five

Get Over
Petty Fears

"We missed you at the retreat this year," I said to my friend at church.

"Oh, I really wanted to come, but I just don't drive on the expressways," she explained.

"You don't?" came my astonished reply. "Why not?

"I just have a fear of expressways, and I couldn't figure how to get to that hotel without driving on an expressway," she told me.

"You mean, you never drive on an expressway? How do you get around this city?" I asked.

She laughed and said, "Well, it's not easy. I just don't go if I have to take an expressway."

How many times has someone—usually a woman—told me what she can't do because of some fear! From fear of flying, to fear of the dark, to fear of speaking in front of a group, to fear of not knowing how to dress for an occasion, I've encountered so many who have missed out on many good things because of what I term a "petty fear."

Fear is a very common enemy for all of us. The Bible is full of admonitions to "fear not," "do not be afraid," "do not be anxious," etc. You can hardly turn a page in Scripture without some reference to fear. Obviously, fear has plagued mankind from the beginning of time. So it's no surprise that fear is something all of us need to "get over."

Fear comes in many shapes and sizes. Some fears are good for us; they prevent us from sticking our hands in a flame, or walking out in traffic, or driving carelessly on icy roads. Of course, the Bible teaches us to fear God, with a reverential awe that should keep us from wandering away from biblical principles.

There are big fears that keep us in bondage and smaller ones that eat around the edges of our happiness and enjoyment of life. Often those larger fears are the result of traumatic experiences or childhood memories that need some special attention and counsel in order for us to be set free from them. I want to address those smaller ones, those petty fears that don't take a rocket scientist to recognize as unnecessary and ones we really need to just "get over."

Fear of a Dreaded Outcome

These are the fears that something bad just might happen, so in order to avoid that possibility we limit our activities and set unnecessary boundaries on our lives. Examples would include:

- Fear of flying

- Fear of driving on expressways

- Fear of driving in cities

- Fear of driving at night

- Fear of going overseas

- Fear of going too far from home

- Fear of eating something different

- Fear of taking any risk

- Fear of any change

In most cases, these kinds of petty fears don't rise to the level of phobias or fixations, but they interfere with our everyday life, they limit where we go and what we do, they keep us from experiences that are often enriching and delightful.

I think of someone who just won't get on an airplane. It's not because she has had a bad experience flying, for she simply has refused to fly. Rather, it is a fear that something bad might happen while she is flying, and so she simply says no to anything that requires a flight.

Where does this fear come from? As is always true, it comes from her thought patterns. Somewhere in her lifetime, probably as a child, someone of influence (could it have been a mother?) has passed this fear of flying down to her, and it has imbedded itself in her mind with such force that she now has a hard-and-fast rule: I don't fly! There's no discussion, no compromise, no consideration whatsoever of what she could do to get over this fear. It is simply: I don't fly.

I am quite certain that she does not consider this a spiritual issue. No doubt she thinks that if she doesn't want to fly, she doesn't have to and it has nothing to do with her relationship with God. She's not breaking any commandments; she's not disobeying God's principles. She simply doesn't want to fly! What's the big deal?

Well, the big deal is that petty fears are a sign that we aren't trusting God in that area. Fear is a red flag indicating lack of faith, lack of trust. And without faith, it's impossible to please God. Fear and faith cannot coexist. Petty fears are symptoms of our refusal to learn to trust a trustworthy God.

I know there are many who truly don't like flying. My niece is not fond of it; she is a white-knuckler, as we say. But she has not allowed it to keep her from flying. She's been to Africa on a missions trip with me, as well as other missions trips and many journeys with her husband and family. Though she never looks forward to flying, she has not allowed it to control her activity. She is "getting over it."

I think of my little dog, Benji. When I had hardwood floors put in my home to replace carpet, he simply refused to climb the stairs because he feared slipping on the wooden floors. It was a change that was uncomfortable to him and he felt insecure. So in order for him to join me on the second floor, he had to be carried up and down the stairs. No amount of cajoling or scolding or encouraging changed his mind; he was not climbing those wooden stairs.

This meant that when I was upstairs and he wanted to be up there with me, he would sit at the bottom of the stairs and whine, and he could whine endlessly! I tried to tell him that it was his fault he was not upstairs with me. He had an unfounded fear of wooden stairs, but words meant nothing to him. Finally, I installed a runner on the wooden stairs and retaught him that he could now navigate the stairs on his own, because there was carpet on the stairs!

That picture of Benji sitting at the bottom of the stairs whining is what I think of when I allow some petty fear to control my movement, my agenda, my lifestyle. I'm sitting there whining because I can't get where I want to be or do what I want to do because of a petty fear. It's far more foolish for me to behave that way than it was for Benji, who had very limited means of reasoning or understanding!

Fear of Change

"That's the way we've always done it" is usually a verbal cover-up for some kind of petty fear. Change can truly bring petty fears out of the closet! Many times we deceive ourselves into thinking that we have very good rational reasons for rejecting change, when actually it's nothing but some fear that just came out of hiding when the possibility of change raised its ugly head.

Fear of change can truly cramp your style, get in your way, trip you up, and keep you down! For example, if you're afraid to learn any new software or new technology, you're going to be left out in the cold quickly because it's changing pretty much as we speak.

I think of Orva Koenigsberg, who came to work for me many years ago when she was in her early seventies. She had never touched a computer, but she informed me that she could learn! So she learned some basic skills, mostly by rote, in order to be able to navigate our then very simple computer software and do the job she needed to do. Orva is in heaven now, but she continues to inspire me with her attitude of "let's do it," never letting fear get in her way.

She told me later that she truly had been afraid of the computer and really didn't want to learn it. But she knew it was a silly fear and she was a determined woman who simply wouldn't allow that fear to hold her back. Because she was able to work for me, and because she had extensive experience in Christian radio, she grew my small radio program from one station in Chicago to being heard on several hundred stations. She was an essential part of the early growth of *The Christian Working Woman* radio program, which would not be where it is today without her knowledge and help. And had she not been willing to learn that computer software and get over her fear of computers, I would not have been able to hire her.

Getting over petty fears doesn't mean that you get rid of the emotion that accompanies these fears. It means you go forward in spite of them:

- You get on that airplane with your knees knocking, but you get on.

- You drive at night, slowly and cautiously with your heart beating a little faster, but you drive.

- You try that new kind of food that you were convinced you'd never like, even if it's only a tiny bite, but you swallow it.

- You say, "Sure, I'll try" when asked to step out of your comfort zone, while you try to hide your shaking hands.

- You agree to a change in procedures, even though you wonder how in the world you'll ever learn to do it differently, but you agree.

Then when you discover that the world did not come crashing down around you, that the earth kept revolving, that your friends are still your friends and your family did not desert you, you begin to realize how truly unfounded and foolish those petty fears really were.

When Benji relearned that he could climb the stairs, he wagged his tail and did a little dance when he got to the top, as I applauded and bragged on him. He had that sense of overcoming a fear, that feeling of accomplishment in not giving into his fear, and he didn't have to sit at the bottom whining any longer.

Get the picture? Once you take that first courageous step to overcome that fear of change, you begin to see new avenues of interest, new opportunities, exciting things to learn and do that were hidden to you while you were in bondage to that petty fear. And conquering fear in one area gives you strength to tackle other areas of petty fears.

Fear of Looking Foolish

I arrived at a church for a speaking engagement one evening, and as I sat down I noticed I had two different shoes on. How could I make such a stupid mistake? How could I get up and make a presentation with unmatched shoes? What would the women think of me? There was no time to go home and change shoes, so I was stuck.

For a miserable few minutes, I was so worried about looking foolish because of my shoes that I truly wondered if I could get it together enough to make my presentation. After those first panic moments, I began to talk to myself: *Good grief, Mary, what's the big deal? So you did something stupid. Do you think you're the first one to make a silly mistake? And your presentation does not depend on your shoes, so get*

75

over it! (By the way, talking to yourself is a very good way to wake yourself up at times like these and force yourself to get over it!)

So, instead of feeling foolish and letting my shoes ruin the purpose for which I was there, I made a joke out of it. The women laughed with me, and the presentation was not impaired because of my foolish feelings.

I have never forgotten this silly incident, for it helped me to realize how foolish it was to let the fear of looking foolish have such control over me. For those of us who are "control freaks" and who base far too much of our self-image on how we look and how together we are, it is really important for us to get over this petty fear for, truly, we look more foolish when we try to avoid looking foolish.

Recently I witnessed a woman who wanted to get her hair cut, but in talking with the hairdresser she expressed a fear that the haircut would not turn out the way she wanted it to. Now we all care about our hair and how it looks, but this woman was really stressed out over whether or not this new haircut would be right for her, and she exhibited an immense amount of fear about whether to get it cut or not. And she wasn't talking about going from very long to very short hair, but whether to cut an inch off or not.

I'm thinking, *It's just a haircut! It will grow back if you don't like it!* But after she left, my hairdresser explained that, because she is a tall woman, she thinks that her hair must not be too short or it will make her look taller. She is afraid that shortening her hair by an inch will draw attention to her height. Watching her reaction, I realized she has a fear of looking foolish and has told herself, no doubt for years, that being tall is a handicap instead of seeing it as a positive attribute, which it is.

I wanted to put my arm around her and say, "Get over it! You're wasting way too much time and emotion on an inch of hair, and the truth is, you are an exceptionally smart-looking tall woman." Of course, I wasn't able to do that, but her fear of looking foolish reminded me of how often I've thought something so small was so important.

Remember, people are not focusing on you nearly as much as you think they are. They are wrapped up in their own world, thinking about themselves, worrying whether they look foolish to you! So get over that needless fear of looking foolish. It's such a waste of time and energy.

Fear of Public Speaking

I have seen studies that show this fear as the number-one fear for many people. Since I've always been a drama queen, loving an audience, I have difficulty relating to this particular fear. But I do understand that it is real for lots of people.

I am in charge of selecting and coaching people in our church to share their stories in our Sunday service. We usually feature one per month, and it always turns out to be the highlight of the service. There is nothing as moving as a personal story of God's grace and love. Stories are powerful teaching tools, which is no doubt why Jesus chose to teach mostly in parables.

More often than not, the person asked to share is not accustomed to speaking in public, and particularly not to a large audience. So quite often the first response to my request is a look of fear in their eyes and a comment such as, "You mean, in front of the whole church?"

Recently a woman who is a medical doctor with impressive credentials and accomplishments—and a wonderful story of God's grace in her life—had this type of reaction. But I assured her that she would never speak to a friendlier audience, and her story would be a great blessing. She agreed to do it in spite of her fear of getting up in front of such a large group.

I think she lost some sleep thinking about it, and the knots were in her stomach that Sunday morning, but she did it. Afterwards, many people responded to her story and told her how meaningful it was to them. She told me how glad she was I had pushed her out of her comfort zone to do this, as she saw how God used it to help others.

It was interesting that, even with all her experience and education, public speaking was still fearful for her. But had she not "gotten over it" and instead refused to share her story, she would have missed a great blessing and many others would have missed the encouragement they received from hearing her story.

My own daughter is not fond of speaking to groups, and a few years ago she was asked to take a leadership role in her church's Bible study program for women. She truly thought she just couldn't take this job because it required her to emcee their weekly Bible studies and that was not her gifting! I encouraged her to believe that God had opened this door for her, that she was the right person for this job, and that God would enable her to do this, even though it was not her cup of tea.

Now, after several years in this leadership position, she recently told me someone had commented on what a good job she did in front of the group, and she was amazed. I'm so glad that her fear of public speaking—a real fear—did not keep her from stepping out of her comfort zone and letting God use her in this way. She has been blessed and she has been a blessing.

The parable of the talents, as found in Matthew 25:14-30 teaches us that when we use what God has given us, He gives us more. When we take the opportunities to serve God even in areas where we're uncomfortable or fearful, He gives us the abilities and skills to do what some petty fear convinced us we could not do. I just wonder how many blessings and opportunities are missed because of this petty fear of speaking in front of a group.

Ephesians 2:10 tells us that... "we are God's handiwork, created in Christ Jesus to do good works, which God prepared in advance for us to do." These good works are the things that bring fulfillment and joy to our lives—they are the avenue to the abundant life Jesus came to give us. So it's really important that we are doing the unique good works God has planned for each of us to do. How many go undone, how has Kingdom work been handicapped, because of some petty fear? It's a clever trick that the enemy uses on too many of us rather effectively.

The Antidote for Fear

We know from Scripture that these petty fears are not from God.

> For God gave us a spirit not of fear but of power and love and self-control. (2 Tim. 1:7, ESV)

"A spirit of fear" is a very accurate description for these petty fears, a feeling of fear that hangs over our heads, raining on our parades and keeping us under its spell. That spirit of fear is not from God; therefore we must conclude it is from our enemy who loves to invade our thought lives with petty fears. It's one of his most successful weapons against us.

So how do we combat these petty fears? If they are indeed petty—small and unnecessary—then we should be able to overcome them. But how?

First, fears have to be exposed; they must be acknowledged for what they are before you will ever get over them. So step one is to name those petty fears; bring them out in the open; write them in your journal. Getting specific is very important. Call them by name!

Just exposing your fear, however, won't solve the problem. Once you've looked it in the eye and faced the fear head-on, you now need a cure for it. And it should not surprise you to learn that the cure for fear is the Word of God. So memorize or put on cards some verses about fear from God's Word. Here is a very small sample of passages in the Bible that address our fears:

> So we say with confidence, 'The Lord is my helper. I will not be afraid. What can man do to me?'(Heb. 13:6)

> Have I not commanded you? Be strong and courageous. Do not be afraid; do not be discouraged, for the LORD your God will be with you wherever you go. (Josh. 1:9)

> When I am afraid, I put my trust in you. (Ps. 56:3)

> In God I trust and am not afraid. What can man do to me? (Ps. 56:11)

> The LORD is with me; I will not be afraid. What can mere mortals do to me? (Ps. 118:6)

> Surely God is my salvation; I will trust and not be afraid. The LORD, the LORD himself, is my strength and my defense; he has become my salvation. (Isa. 12:2)

> But now, this is what the Lord says—he who created you, O Jacob, he who formed you, O Israel: "Fear not,

for I have redeemed you; I have summoned you by name; you are mine. When you pass through the waters, I will be with you; and when you pass through the rivers, they will not sweep over you. When you walk through the fire, you will not be burned; the flames will not set you ablaze." (Isa. 43:1-2)

All of us can memorize Psalm 56:3—one sentence that says, "When I am afraid, I put my trust in you." Use it as a mantra, if need be. Just repeat it over and over, out loud if possible, and keep replacing your thoughts of fear with the truth of God's Word. At the point of the fear, you must choose to put your trust in the Lord and let go of the fear.

In talking with a dear young woman recently, I urged her to use this simple method to combat some unfounded fears she is facing. She has a very teachable spirit, so she did, and within hours she emailed me to say that she had a feeling of peace and a lighter spirit than she had known in weeks. She replaced fear with truth and the truth set her free, as Jesus promised it would in John 8:32.

Learn Perfect Love

John wrote that, "There is no fear in love. But perfect love drives out fear... The one who fears is not made perfect in love" (1 John 4:18). So, those petty fears reveal an area where our love of the Lord is not perfect. Perfect love is synonymous with perfect trust. I can't say I love Jesus with all my heart, soul, and mind if I harbor petty fears. I may love Jesus a lot, but the fear reveals an area where my love for Him is not strong enough, and therefore my faith is weak.

So our challenge is to focus our energy on loving Jesus supremely, making Him Lord in every area of our

81

lives, focusing our thoughts on Him, spending time in His presence, knowing His Word better and better. This will drive out those fears. When we dwell in fear, petty or otherwise, we tend to spend less and less time with Jesus, less and less time in His Word, and more and more time focused on ourselves. That just makes the fear worse and destroys our faith even further.

Getting Over a Petty Fear

A dear, long-time friend just recently told me of how she faced a petty fear. She is the mother of three, grandmother of eight, and for fifty-four years was married to a wonderful man. She is now a widow and, though it's hard, she is using this time in her life to encourage and help others.

When her children were young and she was a stay-at-home mom, she simply refused to drive a car. Her fear of driving had just built up over the years until it was like a mountain that she could not climb. So she said, "No, I don't want to learn to drive." Through all those many years when her children were at home, she could not provide transportation for them. They managed—there were buses to take them to school and friends to hitch a ride with for other occasions. But it was inconvenient at times because Mom didn't drive. Her husband used a truck for work and their car was parked in the garage, so the car was at her disposal. But Gerd was not going to drive it.

When her children were teenagers and going for their driver's license, they would beg her to come along with them. "Come on, Mom; we can get our learner's license and learn together." But there was no persuading her.

One day, at the age of fifty-seven, when the kids were all grown and out of the house, she was taking a walk with a good friend in the neighborhood. This friend had her own fear—the fear of having a mammogram because she was afraid she would learn that she had breast cancer. Her two sisters had breast cancer, and she was most fearful that she would have it too. But instead of doing what she could to find out, she did just the opposite and refused to have a mammogram because she was fearful of learning that she did have cancer.

In talking about their fears that day, Gerd's friend challenged her: "If I make an appointment for a mammogram, will you go get your learner's license?" She said, "Gerd, you can do this with God's help." For some reason—no doubt a "God-thing"—those words got through to Gerd that day and so she took the challenge. The two of them even stopped and shook hands, more or less making a covenant between them. As soon as Gerd got home from the walk, her friend called and said, "I'm picking you up at 10:00 next Wednesday and taking you to get your learner's license. So study the book and be ready."

Gerd felt constrained to be true to her word, so she found one of the books to study for the written test and on the next Wednesday she went for her learner's license. Then she hired a man to give her driving lessons and she learned to drive, eventually got her license, and she is no longer home-bound. Now as a widow this is even more important, because she doesn't have to depend on her friends or family to take her shopping, or go to church, or whatever. As she has gotten over that fear of driving, she has found new freedom. Interestingly, she formed a nice friendship with her driving teacher and was able to share her faith with him in her own unique way.

A Challenge to Get Over Your Petty Fear

Gerd's friend did her a great favor when she challenged her to get her license. Actually, they encouraged each other, and that little bit of push from her friend was enough to help Gerd see that she didn't need to live her entire life afraid to drive. (Interestingly, it took her friend two more years before she went for a mammogram, but with Gerd's continual reminder of their "covenant," she did finally go—and the news was good.)

Is there someone in your life with whom you could make a pact, or someone who would lovingly hold you accountable, to take the first step at getting over your petty fear? Just take the first step and trust God for all the other steps. Depending on how controlling your fear has become, that first step may be to get some Christian counseling to help you make the first step. But why live the rest of your life in bondage to a fear that, by God's grace, you could get over and be free from?

> It is for freedom that Christ has set us free. Stand firm, then, and do not let yourselves be burdened again by a yoke of slavery. (Gal. 5:1)

Christ has come to set you free from every fear. You will be amazed at the freedom that will be yours when you get over your petty fears.

Chapter Six

Get Over
Worrying

The most useless and unproductive thing that most of us do very often is to worry, and unfortunately we can do that anywhere and anytime, employed or unemployed, in school or retired, young or old, single or married—it is universal. It just seems to be the place where our thoughts go when we experience any level of uncertainty or fear or lack of control.

All of us are aware of how worthless and harmful it is to worry, but the challenge is—how do we get over it? Is it really possible to come to a place where we truly don't waste time worrying? And if so, wouldn't that show a lack of concern on our part in some situations? After all, life is full of worrying things, and are we just supposed to be cavalier and nonchalant, as though those things don't bother us at all?

Jesus fully understood our propensity to worry, and He addressed it strongly in His Sermon on the Mount:

> Therefore I tell you, do not worry about your life, what you will eat or drink; or about your body, what you will wear. Is not life more important than food, and the body more important than clothes. Look at the birds of the air; they do not sow or reap or store away in barns, and yet your heavenly Father feeds them. Are you not much more valuable than they? Who of you by worrying can add a single hour to his life? And why do you worry about clothes? See how the lilies of the field grow. They do not labor or spin. Yet I tell you that not even Solomon in all his splendor was dressed like one of these.. . So do not worry, saying, "What shall we eat?" or "What shall we drink?" or "What shall we wear?" For the pagans run after all these things, and your heavenly Father knows that you need them. But seek first his kingdom and his righteousness, and all these things will be given to you as well. Therefore do not worry about tomorrow, for tomorrow will worry about itself. Each day has enough trouble of its own. (Matt. 6:25-29, 31-34)

Since Jesus devoted this much of His Sermon on the Mount to the topic of worrying, we know that it is a common mental trap, and we know that He wants us to get over it. He gave several reasons why we should not worry.

Jesus said that God takes care of little birds, and He asks, "Are you not more valuable than they?" Surely the knowledge of how much God loves us, how deeply He cares for us should cause us to stop worrying. After all, our Heavenly Father is sovereign over everything and everyone in our lives; He is always in control, and because we are His children, He has pledged to take care of our needs. So, that's the first reason that we should not worry—because we are children of God and He never leaves us or forsakes us.

A second reason Jesus tells us not to worry is that it just simply does no good whatsoever. Jesus said, "Who of you by worrying can add a single hour to his life?" Worrying is totally worthless. It never produces any good results, but instead it causes us to lose our peace, to lose our joy, to waste our energy.

We spend lots of emotional and mental energy when we're in worry mode—and has it ever done us one bit of good? No, of course not. Worrying is worthless! You know, most things you are worrying about never happen anyway. Just think back on what you worried about last month or last year? How many of those worries have actually materialized? Worrying probably *contributes* to bad things happening; it certainly doesn't *prevent* them from happening.

Worrying can become a self-fulfilling prophecy. It can be the door we open that allows our worries to materialize. I remember talking with a woman who was scheduled to have a performance review on her job, and she was worried that she would get a bad review and, therefore, not get a raise. She told me all the reasons she was convinced that her boss would not do right by her. I told her that if she continued to worry about this matter and continued to prophesy disaster, it would affect the way she behaved; her negative attitude would show in ways she couldn't imagine, and her very worrying could cause her to have a poor review.

Jesus gives us another really strong reason not to worry: It is a poor testimony to those around us. In verse 32, we read: "For the pagans run after all these things, and your heavenly Father knows that you need them." Jesus is talking about material things, and He told His disciples that those who are not believers are always worrying about these things.

Isn't it true that most of the people around you are worrying? Just think about the conversations you have with people, particularly people who are not yet believers in Jesus Christ. You'll observe that they are worrying a lot. So if those of us who are disciples of Jesus Christ worry just like everyone else, what kind of testimony is that? And you can be sure that when you are worrying, people know it because you talk about it, it shows on your face and in your body language, and it's not particularly attractive.

Jesus said that we should not worry about tomorrow. It's true that most of our worries are about tomorrow. *What's going to happen? What if this happens or that doesn't happen?* We allow our minds to conjure up all kinds of possible scenarios that frighten us and worry us. Jesus knew this and He specifically tells us not to worry about tomorrow, not to borrow trouble from tomorrow.

I know some friends who are trying to make a decision about a major move in their lives—moving from one place to another and altering their current lifestyle dramatically. As I talked with them, I realized that they were considering this move based on being fearful of tomorrow, trying to make sure that nothing bad will happen in the future. Obviously, we should be properly wise in preparing for the future, but there's no way any of us can know what the future holds. Worrying about the future, making decisions out of fear, goes against this simple directive from our Lord—not to worry about tomorrow.

The ideal woman is described in Proverbs 31 as a woman who can "laugh at the days to come" (v. 25). She is a woman of faith who simply refuses to let her fears of tomorrow hold her captive through worry and fear.

Just imagine that you're a mom or dad with a six-year-old child and, because you love your child, you take care of her. She always has plenty to eat, nice clothes to wear, a roof over her head, her health needs cared for, her safety provided—everything a parent should do you have willingly and lovingly done for your child. Now suppose every morning this same child gets up crying, despondent, and worried. And every morning she comes to you and says, "What am I going to eat today? I'm worried about whether or not you'll have food for me today. And what about my clothes? Will I have anything to wear today? Are you going to stay with me today or are you going to leave me? What if something bad happens to me; will you be there to help me?"

If your precious child did that, it would be offensive to you, would it not? How could she doubt that you would continue to take care of her as you always have done? Why can't she just trust you to do what is best for her? You always have and yet she simply doesn't trust you.

The example is rather ridiculous, since children typically don't worry about those basic things—at least not if they are cared for as they should be. And yet, as children of God, isn't that what we do to God when we worry about anything? It must be offensive to Him when He sees us worrying, because worry is always an indication that we're not trusting God in whatever we're worrying about.

Worry is like the check engine light in your car. You know when that light goes on that something is wrong with your car and you need to have it checked out. Well, when you and I are worrying, it's a warning light that something is wrong with us spiritually. Either we've forgotten who we are in Christ and how our heavenly Father has promised to take care of us, or our faith is very weak, perhaps because we've not spent enough time in the Word of God, or we're not truly seeking first God's kingdom. Other things, other people, other activities have taken first place in our lives.

Worrying is totally worthless, but even more than that, worrying is faithless! I just don't think we often put worry into the category of "sin," do we? We worry and worry and never think to apologize to God and repent of this sin of worrying. Paul wrote that "anything that does not come from faith is sin" (Rom. 14:23b). Well, for sure, worrying does not come from faith. Faith and worry are like oil and water; they don't mix. Therefore, continually worrying about anything is a sin.

Certainly, there are things that will and should concern us. The difference between a worry and a concern is the way we handle them. The situation that is causing you to worry may indeed be a true concern, but responding by worrying just makes it worse. Take those true concerns— that child who is sick, that parent who is showing signs of dementia, that job interview coming up, that unexpected expense, that difficult boss you work for, that mate who does not share your faith in Christ—take those true concerns and cast them on Jesus. He invites us to do this:

Come to me, all you who are weary and burdened, and I will give you rest. Take my yoke upon you and learn from me, for I am gentle and humble in heart, and you will find rest for your souls. For my yoke is easy and my burden is light. (Matt. 11:28-30)

If your burden of worry is heavy, then you're carrying the wrong burden. Jesus' burden is light; it's a burden, a concern, but it's not going to weigh you down and keep you from joy and peace. Yes, life hits us with serious concerns that we cannot ignore; we are not to live in denial. But we are to cast all our cares on Jesus, because He cares for us.

How to Get Over Worrying

If we truly want to get over worrying, the first thing we need to do is to confess our worrying sins. What do you worry about most? Here are some common ones:

- How to pay the bills

- How to find a job

- How to keep a job

- How to find a mate

- How to find a cure

- How to control someone

- How to change a situation

What is on your list? I encourage you to ask God to forgive you for anything you worry about and be specific. That's a good first step in getting over worthless worries.

Worry is a function of your mind, your thoughts. In order to stop worrying, you have to change your thought patterns. And in order to change your thought patterns, you have to replace wrong thoughts with right thoughts. So here is one guaranteed replacement thought that can stop you from worrying:

You have a heavenly Father who is taking care of you.

Jesus said in Matthew 6 that our heavenly Father knows what we need and will provide for our needs when we seek first His kingdom and His righteousness. If we truly believe that the God of all creation cares about us individually and has committed Himself to provide what we need and to make all things work for our good, those thoughts will drive out worry. The challenge we face is to literally replace the worries with these good thoughts.

You can do that with inspirational music, by quoting Scripture, by reading something inspirational, or having a conversation with someone who will help you replace your worrying thoughts with God's truth.

Recently I received a phone call from a new believer, a person who is totally sincere about following Christ but is struggling with a relationship issue that is keeping her mired in worry. She was having a very bad day because of the response she had received from this other person and was again very worried about how it would all turn out. At that moment she needed something to get her out of that pit of worry.

After reminding her of how much God loves her, I suggested that she had to take immediate steps to change her thought patterns. She needed to sit down quietly and read something helpful, such as some of the Psalms. I told her to put on some good music, uplifting music, and sing along. I think it was the first time she realized that her very worried state of mind was something she could actually change by taking control of her thought patterns and refusing to allow her mind to dwell in worry.

However, when you and I are in worry mode, the moment of taking those thoughts captive and making them obedient to Christ, as we read in 2 Corinthians 10:5, is like arm-wrestling. It is a fight; it's a tug of war between our natural tendency to worry and our desire to let go of our worries and truly trust Christ. Don't be surprised to discover that the doing is harder than the saying. This is when you cry for help to the Lord and rely on His strength to do what you can't do. Philippians 4:13 reminds us that we can do everything through Christ who gives us strength.

Also, that decision to take those worrying thoughts captive may last only a brief time, like five minutes or an hour. So you just repeat the process. You are building spiritual muscle and the more you practice, the sooner you'll have the victory over worry. Don't be discouraged that you find yourself going back to the worry pit. Just refuse to stay there, by God's grace, and you'll begin to recognize how much nicer life is when you're not consumed with worry.

I hope you will remember that worrying is worthless and determine by God's grace to get over it, one worry at a time, and live in the peace and comfort of knowing God is in control of your life and of the universe!

Chapter Seven

Get Over
Unrealistic
Expectations

Ask almost any parent what they want for their child, and the answer will usually be some version of "I just want him/her to be happy." I admit I want my daughter and son-in-law to be happy. Happiness— which has different meanings to different people—seems to be the gold medal of life for which most people are striving. After all, doesn't the U.S. Constitution guarantee us the right to be happy?

Well, no, happiness is not guaranteed to us by the Constitution. It is not our birthright to be happy. The Constitution says we have the right to *pursue* happiness. If by happiness you mean the absence of anything unpleasant, and total satisfaction with the circumstances of your life, then, for sure, no one on this earth has ever achieved continual happiness. It is an unrealistic expectation.

Those who expect life to deliver a continual stream of satisfaction and contentment live in a world of disappointment. Those who take what life delivers, make lemonade out of lemons, and find joy in the moment—who have gotten over their unrealistic expectations—find that elusive state of "being content in any and every situation" which the apostle Paul referred to in Philippians 4:12. Paul said he had "learned to be content whatever the circumstances" (v. 11b). It had to be learned even by this giant of a Christian. That encourages me, because I know that being content with my circumstances does not come naturally or easy for me. Just as we have to study algebra or calculus in order to understand it, we need to enroll in Contentment 101 and learn to be content. But it won't happen until we decide to enroll.

Getting over unrealistic expectations is one of the best gifts you'll ever give yourself. It will reduce your stress and enhance your joy more than you can imagine, and it will set you free from the bondage of expecting from people and things what they cannot or will not deliver. And the good news is, you have control over your expectation levels. So much of our lives is outside of our control, but this is not.

Common Areas of Unrealistic Expectations

Can you recall the last time you were sorely disappointed by something or someone? Disappointment is always caused by our expectations not being met—that's the definition of it. So what expectation did you have that was not fulfilled and therefore caused you to be disappointed? It could be something as simple as you expected the weather to be good for a special event and instead it rained. Or something far more significant—you expected someone to fulfill a promise made to you and he/she did not.

Let's look at some of the most common areas where we tend to have unrealistic expectations; why that happens to us so frequently; and what the Bible says about overcoming this joy-stealer.

Unrealistic Expectations of People

Undoubtedly our most common unrealistic expectations are the ones we have of other people. Most relationship struggles are created by our expectations not being met, and when those expectations are unrealistic, it puts a strain on that relationship that can be deadly.

All too often women think that husbands are going to make them happy all the time. They believe that a husband will speak their "love language," whether that be daily showers of words of love, gifts and celebrations, acts of service without being asked—or whatever. Then they discover that their expectations of what a husband should be and do are not on the same page as their husband's idea of what is required of him. And the tugs of war begin, leading to nagging, tears, angry words, etc. In a word, disappointment. Of course, it works the other way too. Men are prone to think their wives should always look lovely, cook great meals, maintain a spotless home, be supportive of them—whatever their idea of the perfect wife might be. And before long they discover that their expectations are not met.

We single women can be possessed with the expectation that getting married is our doorway to completeness, and we develop very unrealistic ideas of what marriage will do for us. For ten long years, I made the pursuit of a husband my highest priority, believing that life would never be happy without one (there we go again with our pursuit of happiness). At one point, I had a relationship with a very nice man and thought my happiness totally depended on him asking me to marry him. But I look back now and realize that I had incredibly unrealistic expectations of what he would be able to do for me. I was so desperate to find a man that I simply overlooked any problems I saw, and focused only on my needs and how I thought he would meet every one of them.

I think he saw the problem better than I did. On one occasion, he said to me, "Mary, I'd love to be the open person you are, but I can never be that way." I wanted him to share his every thought with me and I just knew if we got married, he'd be able to do that and we could be so close. But that would never have happened. It didn't happen then and marriage surely wouldn't have made it happen. Yet I had that totally unrealistic expectation of him, and I would have been sorely disappointed had we married.

We women—and I'm sure men too—tend to conjure up in our minds what a mate should and could be, and many times we have very unrealistic expectations of what they're able to deliver. Then we discover, sometimes too late, that it's not going to happen, and life becomes very dreary and disappointing because we expected much more than we should have. No doubt unrealistic expectations are the basic cause of many failed marriages.

We also can expect too much of our children. How many mothers have thought that the darling little baby they wanted so desperately would fulfill all their needs and make them totally complete and happy, only to discover that those little babies pitch temper tantrums, get sick and cry all night, and grow up into something less than the straight-A students they had imagined. When we set up unrealistic expectations of our children, not only will we be disappointed, but we're likely to make life pretty difficult for them.

How often have you been disappointed by a friend or relative who didn't come through for you when you needed her or him? You were crushed to realize that this dear friend didn't seem to notice or care about your problem, just when you needed that person the most. Not that long ago, I allowed myself to wallow in self-pity for an evening because I felt overlooked and neglected by a family member. Thankfully, my pity parties don't come too often anymore or last too long, as I've finally learned how miserable those parties are—and nobody comes! But nonetheless, I expected something truly unrealistic and made myself miserable for a few hours as a result.

People disappoint us—from parents and relatives, to husbands and children, co-workers and managers, friends and family. We expect more than they deliver, and therefore our happiness is affected because they don't live up to our expectations. Obviously we have a right to expect certain things from the people in our lives, such as love and care from our parents, loyalty and support from our mates, etc. When our realistic and justifiable expectations go unmet, then the resultant effects can be traumatic and lasting. But I'm referring to our unrealistic expectations—where we have been disappointed because we held the bar too high and didn't put ourselves in the other person's shoes.

Dear friends, there is no person on earth who can deliver on every promise and be everything we want him or her to be. People will always disappoint us; that's because we're all sinners and the best of us fail miserably at times. If you've been living with unrealistic expectations of the people in your life, please get over it! Yes, for their sakes, but just as importantly, for your own sake. It is self-imposed misery to continually expect of others what they cannot deliver and what we should not expect them to deliver.

It should also be noted that there are times when we have to face the fact that our reasonable expectations are not going to be met and decide how to deal with it. Sometimes painful decisions have to be made because of unmet realistic expectations. For example, remaining faithful in marriage was promised during that wedding ceremony and no one should have to live with an unfaithful mate. I've known people who have been faced with this major disappointment in a mate and decided it was of brief duration, there was true repentance and sorrow, and they have been able to restore the marriage, as difficult as that was to do. Others have faced a pattern of infidelity in their mate and been forced to separate or divorce because it is not unrealistic to expect faithfulness in marriage. The variations on this theme are myriad, but it just makes the point that not all expectations are unrealistic and no one should be expected to tolerate certain disappointments.

But you may discover that one of your expectations of your mate is not being met—such as going to church with you—and while that is a good and realistic expectation, it is an example of one that you should live with rather than allow it to ruin your marriage. I think of many couples I know where this is the situation, and for some there have been happy endings where, after sometimes many years and lots of prayer, the mate has changed and is now in church regularly. I have a dear friend who married a man who did not share her faith in God and she knew that, but she believed—as so many women have done—that he would "see the light" after they were married and become a believer. They were married for over fifty years, and he never went to church with her. He did profess a belief in Jesus just before his death, but she lived their entire married life going to church by herself and raising her children in her faith without the support of her husband.

Unrealistic Expectations of Things

Money and what it can buy have always claimed to be our gateway to security, contentment, fulfillment, success. They clamor for our allegiance, making promises that cannot be fulfilled. And yet our addiction to owning things grows at an alarming pace. No doubt our media-saturated culture contributes to the addiction. But it's nothing new. Jesus warned us about it:

> No one can serve two masters. Either he will hate the one and love the other, or he will be devoted to the one and despise the other. You cannot serve both God and Money. (Matt. 6:24)

During my ten-year hiatus from God's control of my life, I thought that status symbols would fulfill me, so I accumulated clothes and things to impress people and myself. When I moved to Chicago, I bought a large, nice condo, even though it stretched me financially to do so. I thought living in that nice place would make me happy. I unrealistically expected things to fill up the empty space inside of me.

Have you been thinking: "If only I had this, then I would be happy"? Is it a certain house, a new car, designer clothes, a fancy vacation? If/when you get them, they'll make you feel good for about one or two days, if you're like most of us. And then the glow wears off and you feel empty again.

I remember having lunch with a woman who was searching for happiness. She had just bought a very expensive dress and was telling me about it, while at the same time telling me how unhappy she was with her life. I asked her, "Does your new dress make you happy?" She shook her head despondently and said, "No." I could understand her because I did the same kind of dumb things for many years.

Unrealistic expectations of things and possessions will cause you to be a slave to those things, and you'll keep trying to get more and more to fill up the emptiness. But they never will.

Unrealistic Expectations of our Jobs

Many people are continually unhappy with their jobs because they expect to have a job that is always challenging and exciting. I think of one woman I knew who changed jobs about once a year. She would stay in a job until it disappointed her in some way or another, and then start looking for the perfect job again. Of course, she never found the perfect job and, because of those unrealistic expectations, she lived in perpetual frustration.

As one who has spent many years in the workplace, I can tell you that you'll have moments when the job is exciting and fulfilling, but they are just that: moments. Catch them and enjoy them, but don't expect to find a job without dull and boring days.

Unrealistic Expectations of Ourselves

They tell us that one of the chief causes of suicides is that people expect too much of themselves. Try as hard as we might, we are not super-people, we cannot please everyone, and we will fail to live up to our own expectations and standards at times. This doesn't mean that we let ourselves off the hook easily and justify our failures and weaknesses with the "That's just the way I am" excuse. But if you are your own worst critic and you never give yourself a break, you will live in a world of disappointment.

The Psalmist wrote: "He knows how we are formed, he remembers that we are dust" (Ps. 103:14). God knows how frail we are at best, and yet some of us never can accept our less-than-perfect condition. As the years have passed, I have gradually come to a place of accepting my failures without wallowing in self-accusations. I think it happens as we become more confident of the firm ground we are on with our Creator and Savior, Jesus Christ. One of the most important truths of the gospel is that Jesus knows the worst about us and loves us still. We are assured as children of God that nothing can separate us from His love, and that includes our worst days, our repeated failures, our numerous imperfections.

One of my favorite classics is *Knowing God* by J.I. Packer, and I have this quote from his book written in my prayer journal to remind me of this marvelous truth:

> There is tremendous relief in knowing that His love to me is utterly realistic, based at every point on prior knowledge of the worst about me, so that no discovery now can disillusion Him about me, in the way I am so often disillusioned about myself, and quench His determination to bless me. There is, certainly, great cause for humility in the thought that He sees all the twisted things about me that my fellow-men do not see (and am I glad!), and that He sees more corruption in me

than that which I see in myself, (which, in all conscience, is enough). There is, however, equally great incentive to worship and love God in the thought that, for some unfathomable reason, He wants me as His friend, and desires to be my friend, and has given His Son to die for me in order to realize this purpose.[1]

The more I am immersed in this truth through study of the Bible and continual growth in my trust in the God who created me, the less shocked I am to discover my own imperfections and failures, the more motivated I am to allow His Spirit to change me in those areas, and the less time I spend beating myself up because I didn't live up to my own expectations. It is a paradoxical truth that by accepting my own weaknesses and recognizing my own inability to be everything I should be, the more I am able to allow the power of the risen Christ to live out His life in me and cause me to bear much fruit.

Jesus was aware of His disciples' inability to be perfect. Even at the time He needed them most, they failed Him as He asked them to pray with Him in the Garden of Gethsemane. Do you remember what He said, as He found them sleeping instead of praying? "'Could you men keep not watch with me for one hour?' he asked Peter. 'Watch and pray so that you will not fall into temptation. The spirit is willing, but the body is weak'" (Matt. 26:40b-41).

In the thirteenth chapter of 1 Corinthians, Paul reminds us that "we know in part and we prophesy in part, but when perfection comes, the imperfect disappears ... Now we see but a poor reflection as in a mirror; then we shall see face to face. Now I know in part; then I shall

---

1   J.I. Packer, *Knowing God*, InterVarsity Press, 1973, p. 37.

know fully, even as I am fully known" (1 Cor. 13:9-10, 12). Perfection hasn't come for us yet; it's something that a follower of Christ can look forward to, but not in this human body on this sinful earth.

We keep thinking *If only I were smarter*, or *if only I were thinner. If only I had more talent*, or *if only I could accomplish something great.* Barbra Minar writes:

> Thinking we should be flawless is a devastatingly unrealistic expectation. A real joy stealer! This ideal is promoted through the messages we receive from parents, peers, schools, and church. Trying to be perfect can lead us to:
>
> - dishonesty (We have to lie to be 'nice' and keep everyone happy.)
>
> - illusion (We have to stay in control to be perfect.)
>
> - denial (We cannot let ourselves know we have made mistakes.)
>
> - defensiveness (We cannot let others show us our mistakes.)
>
> The bottom line is that perfectionists live in fear—fear of being their real, imperfect selves.[2]

There are many people today who are always unhappy, never satisfied, and continually despondent because they can't be everything they think they should be. They compare themselves with others and come up short. They set unrealistic goals that cannot be met, and then they feel like failures.

---

2   Barbra Goodyear Minar, *Unrealistic Expectations*, SP Publications, Inc. 1990, p. 58

Why We Have Unrealistic Expectations

Where do our unrealistic expectations originate? First, we've been fed erroneous information from the world around us about what we should expect from people and things. I think our enemy gets into the act here and feeds us this information to get us off-track. These messages come through the media, through other people, and through our own out-of-control imaginations.

Secondly, we come up with these unrealistic expectations when we start to compare ourselves with others. You expect your husband to be like someone else's husband, your child to perform like another child, your boss to treat you like your friend's boss treats her, etc. Comparison is one real cause of unrealistic expectations (See Chapter 2).

Third, some of us have been shaped by our parents to expect too much of ourselves. If your parents were never satisfied with what you did or how you performed, if they always found fault with your accomplishments no matter how hard you worked or tried, you've probably come to expect too much of yourself and never been able to enjoy your achievements very much because of it.

And then we look for our expectations and needs to be met in the wrong place. That need for acceptance and love that is so deep in each of us can be met, but we have to go to the right source.

Finding Victory Over Unrealistic Expectations

How can we avoid the tendency to expect too much of other people: of our parents, our mates, our children, our friendships? What can we do to keep from setting ourselves up for failure and disappointment because we have unrealistic expectations of possessions, of parenting, of marriage, of careers, of ourselves—of life itself?

Here's one practical suggestion that has helped me. Become intentional about enjoying the little things that come your way. Many times we're looking for big doses of happiness and miss all the other small things that we can enjoy. Smell those flowers along the way. Relish the beautiful weather when you have it. Dote on the cute thing your child just did. Rejoice with the success your friend has had. Look in the mirror and remind yourself that you are "fearfully and wonderfully made," as we read in Psalm 139:14. Enjoy the everyday blessings that we so easily overlook. You'll find that life is not nearly so disappointing when you expect less from it and enjoy what it delivers.

And then, of course, we have to learn to appreciate what we do have and dismiss from our minds what we don't have. Your husband doesn't tell you he loves you enough? Sorry about that, but surely he does something right! Focus on that. There was something that made you marry him and you may have lost your focus on the good things. Who knows, there may be other women looking at you with envy, wishing their husband was like yours!

Your wife isn't as supportive and encouraging as you wish she were? That's too bad, but think about the things about her that you do admire. Is she good with budgeting money? Count your blessings and thank her for that.

Your child is not making the best grades in school? Be thankful that he or she is not on drugs, has made good friends, etc. My best friend, Fran, was always a help to me in this way as our children were growing up. When she was having some problem with one of her kids, I tried to remind her of the good things about them and help her get her perspective back, and she did that for me too.

Your job is not so challenging? Well, what are the good things about it? For one thing, you have a job and that's a blessing, especially in these challenging economic times. Maybe the salary is not what you think it should be, but then it pays your bills and keeps you going. Think about how good it is not to be job-hunting!

You'll recognize that this is the principle of Philippians 4:8—think positively about what you do have.

> Finally, brothers, whatever is true, whatever is noble, whatever is right, whatever is pure, whatever is lovely, whatever is admirable—if anything is excellent or praiseworthy—think about such things.

If you're living with lots of unrealistic expectations, undoubtedly you're allowing yourself to think incorrectly— to focus on what's missing rather than on what you have. So many people get caught in this trap and make their lives very miserable as a result.

When we set our life's focus on knowing and pleasing God, we will not be disappointed. Jesus Christ is the one person who can always deliver on His promises, and I guarantee you, if you search for Him with your whole heart, He will meet your expectations.

There's an old chorus I sing often, which says:

> There's no disappointment in Jesus,

> He's all that He promised to be.

> His love and His care comfort me everywhere.

> He is no disappointment to me.

For ten long years I looked to people, things, and careers to fulfill me. My expectations for myself were great as well.

And I never found what I was looking for. But some years ago, I turned back to the Lord and have since focused my life on knowing Him.

Believe me, I haven't done it all right in those years, but I have kept the focus on Jesus, and the difference is like night and day. My circumstances haven't basically changed—I'm still a single mom now with many more years under my belt. But as I've raised my expectations of what I needed in Jesus, and lowered my expectations of what people and things could do for me, I have found joy and contentment.

If you've never experienced that in your life, it's either because you don't truly know Him as your Lord and Savior, or you're looking to other things and people to meet your needs, and not spending time getting to know Jesus.

I encourage you today to get over your unrealistic expectations by fixing your desires on Jesus Christ. As He fills you up, the other things that don't live up to your expectations will not affect your joy and your contentment nearly as much, because Jesus promises, "Never will I leave you; never will I forsake you" (Heb. 13:5b), and He can and will keep that promise. There's no disappointment in Jesus, and the more you make that truth a reality in your life, the better you will be able to get over your unrealistic expectations.

Chapter Eight

Get Over
Putting Yourself
in a Box

What *do you want to be when you grow up?* That's a familiar question that most young children are asked at various stages and ages, and you'll hear answers like *a doctor, a fireman, a teacher, an astronaut*— whatever! I just wonder how many people actually fulfill those childhood dreams when they grow up. Children are far more likely to "think outside the box" than we grown-ups are, don't you agree?

When I was a young career woman, the world was just beginning to open to women to pursue any career or job for which they were qualified. No longer were doors closed to us; it became illegal to prohibit a woman from a job just because she was a woman. I had choices that were not available to women in former generations. But women had been in those limited boxes for so long that it was difficult for many of us to see ourselves outside those boxes.

Today you would be hard-pressed to find any job or occupation where women are not involved and in most cases flourishing. My first job in sales had been closed to women previously under the pretense that women could not carry the heavy equipment! Well, not only could we do that, we could carry heavy sales quotas and excel in that position. Not only did we women then have the benefit of those new careers, but the companies that hired us profited very nicely from having us on board.

Ask yourself what box or boxes you have put yourself in. Here are some common ones:

- I'm too old to do that—or too young

- I don't have the right education

- I don't have the right experience

- I don't have enough money

- I can't carry a tune

- I'm not good at mathematics

- I'm not good with people

- I'm too shy to do that

- I'll never be able to learn all this

- I don't have the right looks

- I'm too big—or I'm too small!

- That's not my gift

This list is virtually endless. You may be in your own unique box. Think about it: what have you been telling yourself you cannot do for some reason like this? It's time to get over it!

Ephesians 2:10 says: "For we are God's handiwork, created in Christ Jesus to do good works, which God prepared in advance for us to do." I'm convinced that many of us are missing out on the good works God prepared for us to do because we've allowed others to put us in a box or, more likely, we've put ourselves in some boxes, and we just can't believe that God wants us out of the box and will equip us to do what He intended from the beginning of time for us to do.

I have a nephew who has a dream to be a Major League baseball player. He pours his heart and soul into preparing himself to pursue this dream. Everything he can do to improve his skills, he is doing. I know he is discouraged at times, but he just won't give up his dream. I don't know if he'll ever make it to the Major Leagues, but I know that by pursuing his dream, he's never going to look back and regret that he didn't try. And in the pursuit, he is learning discipline and hard work, and developing a "never-give-up" character, so that wherever God takes him, he will benefit from pursuing his dream.

Proverbs 29:18 (KJV) says: "Where there is no vision, the people perish." If you've never had a vision of what you could do, if you've never aspired to something so big that it scared you, then you may be perishing on the vine. In the parable of the talents, Jesus taught us the principle that if we don't use what He gives us, not only will He not give us more, we will lose what we have! (See Matt. 25:14-30.) Without a vision, we begin to shrivel up and settle for mediocrity. That inward deterioration occurs subtly and could go unnoticed, even by yourself, but eventually it catches up with you when you begin to see your life as humdrum or boring or meaningless.

From Passion to Vision to Ministry

After I came back to the Lord and made Jesus the Lord of my life, a passion began to grow in me. I didn't know it was a passion; I didn't call it a passion. I just couldn't get it off my mind. And that passion was to minister to women like me—women who went into the workplace regularly. I started where I was, with a Monday-night Bible study in my home. This was over thirty years ago, but, if I remember correctly, I just asked a few career women like myself who lived pretty near me in Chicago to come for a Bible study.

Mind you, I wasn't a very experienced teacher. I didn't have any materials to use except God's Word. I had never taken a course in how to begin a small group. But I knew there were women like me who needed help and encouragement. So six or seven women began to come to my home on Monday evenings. I taught, we prayed, and we became a support group for each other. Some of my sweetest memories in ministry go back to that small group, and the women in that group are still so very dear to me. This lasted several years.

Then I realized that my church, located in the heart of a large city, didn't have any kind of a ministry for workplace women, and the church was full of career women. So I expressed my "passion" to my pastor and he encouraged me to start a ministry. Another woman and I put together a plan, took it to the elders for approval, and began what we called Women in the Working World—a Saturday, monthly luncheon. We began with twenty or so women and it grew to be over 300 women who could come once a month for encouragement and fellowship. It lasted in this format for over twenty years.

I wouldn't even want to have tapes of those first years of my ministry at these luncheons. I can only imagine how inept I was as a speaker, how much I had to learn about programing, how many mistakes I made along the way. But I kept going.

Then I listened to Christian radio and never heard anyone talking about my lifestyle and me. It was as though Christian women were not in the workplace—or maybe they shouldn't be. This didn't seem right to me, so I began to pray about a radio program for working women on Christian stations. I knew nothing about radio; I had not the vaguest idea what it would take to start a radio ministry; I didn't even know anyone in Christian radio. But the passion would not go away. So I prayed about it for about eighteen months. I remember feeling weird praying about something that I was so totally unqualified to do and so ignorant of. But I couldn't get it off my mind.

Finally, on the way to work one morning, after again praying about starting a radio program, I remember thinking, "You've prayed about this a long time. Maybe it's time to do something. I wonder how you start a radio program?" I determined that I would do some research and find out how to start a Christian radio program.

On that very day as I arrived at work, there was a newspaper on my desk with an article about a new Christian radio station in Chicago. That caught my attention. I thought, "I wonder if this is the station I am supposed to be on." So I determined to give them a call and ask some questions. But on that very day, before I could call them, they called me and asked me to be on a talk show coming up on the feminist movement.

Where they got my name I still don't know. I had no name recognition. But I didn't figure that was a coincidence; so when I went to do the talk show, I told a woman who worked at the station about my idea for this program. She encouraged me to move ahead on it; I asked some questions, and started the ball rolling to make it a reality. This was in May of 1984 and by August I was on that one station on Saturday mornings at 8:45 for fifteen minutes. A friend came along to do the announcing for me, we recorded four programs at a time, and that's how it started.

I believe God placed a passion in my heart and since it would not go away, even though it took me way out of my box, the passion became a vision, God opened some doors, and the vision became this radio ministry which, as I write, is in its twenty-seventh year. There is a Monday-through-Friday edition of *The Christian Working Woman*, as well as the weekend edition which began in 1984, and now we're heard on about five hundred Christian stations nationally and internationally.

God deals with all of us in unique ways and I don't share my experience as a model of how it will work for anyone else. But what will work for a person who has a vision of what God wants you to do and is willing to step out of whatever boxes you are in, is that God will guide you step by step and will lead you to new avenues of service that just shatter all the stereotypes and boxes that you or anyone else has tried to impose upon you.

Philippians 1:6 says: "Being confident of this, that he who began a good work in you will carry it on to completion until the day of Christ Jesus." God won't give you a vision or a passion and then mock you or frustrate you. If it is of God, you can be confident that He began it and He will carry it on to completion. It may take more time than you thought it would; it may look a little different than you imagined; but if it is of God and He puts it in your heart, all you have to do is just take the next step! He'll guide you each step of the way.

Is It of God?

How do you know if this passion or vision is a God-thing or not? That's a good question and one you definitely need to pursue. You may need counsel from some wise people, or research, or just time to pray about it a lot and make sure you're not running down your own path and simply expecting God to bless your plans.

Here are seven signs that I believe will help you answer this question:

Sign Number 1: It won't go away.

If God has a plan that will take you out of your comfort zone—out of some box you're in—it will not go away. And as you pray about it (and that must be step number one!), it will get stronger, not weaker.

Believe me, I've had lots of other "passions" and ideas that I thought at first were something God wanted me to pursue, but it didn't take long for those things to fade in my mind. I remember at one point I thought God was leading me in a certain direction, so I began to talk to some people, make some moves, ask some questions, and then I realized that I was working so hard to try to make this happen, there was no joy in it, and I really didn't want

117

to do it anyway after a while. If you have to keep pushing the doors open and there is resistance on every hand, most of the time it's because God is saying either "No, not that" or "No, not now."

Of course, we have to be persistent and not give up at the first obstacle, but if it's of God, it won't go away in your heart. Instead it will grow and, even though it looks impossible, you just won't be able to get away from it.

Sign Number 2: Your motivation will be to serve God and others.

God doesn't give us passions or visions just to make us feel good about ourselves or help us achieve our personal goals. If it's from God you will be motivated out of a love for God and for people, and it will be all about serving. There will be sacrifice involved on your part; it will require you to give of yourself in new ways.

This passage from Isaiah 58:6-8 is becoming one of my favorites:

> Is not this the kind of fasting I have chosen: to loose the chains of injustice and untie the cords of the yoke, to set the oppressed free and break every yoke? Is it not to share your food with the hungry and to provide the poor wanderer with shelter—when you see the naked, to clothe him, and not to turn away from your own flesh and blood? Then your light will break forth like the dawn, and your healing will quickly appear; then your righteousness will go before you, and the glory of the Lord will be your rearguard.

Remember what Jesus told us in Mark 9:35: "Sitting down, Jesus called the Twelve and said, 'Anyone who wants to be first must be the very last, and the servant of all.'"

God's vision for your life will lead you to become a servant, in one way or another. Are you ready for that?

Sign Number 3: There will be a need for it.

God is not inefficient and He does things "in a fitting and orderly way" (1 Cor. 14:40). If God is leading you out of your box, it's because someone needs you out of that box, doing what God has for you to do. It won't be a whimsical flight of your imagination. It won't be because you just want to do something creative or different. It will be to meet a need.

Sign Number 4: God will open doors for you and confirm it through His Word.

If this vision is a God-thing, you won't have to push and shove, and beg and plead. You will have to be persistent, but God will open some doors for you and confirm in some ways that this is of Him. You will see some small and/or large miracles as God opens these doors. You will be amazed, frightened, awestruck, and excited.

I remember when I began to see that my radio ministry was not just for this one station in Chicago. I had been mentored and encouraged to enlarge my vision and take the program to other Christian stations. I don't frighten easily, but as I began to think about growing this radio ministry, I was scared. This was way bigger than anything I had ever thought it would be and I would need resources that I didn't have. So I said, "Lord, I need confirmation from Your Word that this is of You, or I'm not going to do it. Give me clear guidance, please."

My reading that day was in Isaiah 50. (I didn't just plop open the Bible and expect something to jump off the page, but followed my normal reading plan.) Verses four and seven simply hit me between the eyes that day:

> The Sovereign Lord has given me an instructed tongue, to know the word that sustains the weary ... Because the Sovereign Lord helps me, I will not be disgraced. Therefore have I set my face like flint, and I know I will not be put to shame.

There was no doubt in my mind that these two verses were God's voice to me, His promise to me, and His green light to enlarge my ministry. I can't tell you how many times in the past years I've gone back to that passage. It is framed and hanging over my desk, and I've hung on to that promise from God through these years, remembering that He has promised I will not be put to shame as I set my face like flint to do the good thing He prepared for me to do.

When you get out of your comfortable box and start pursuing the passion God has given you, you need a promise from His Word to hang on to. Ask God for it. It's there for you.

Sign Number 5: Your spiritual leader(s) will counsel and/or encourage you.

All of us need and should have those people in our lives who are our spiritual leaders, and for the most part, that should come through our church leaders. The local church is God's structure, His method of accountability and teaching. All of us need to be in a church where the truth is taught and where we have godly leadership. There may also be other wise people in our lives whom we trust to give us godly counsel and who will speak the truth in love to us.

Not all of our visions will require support or approval from our church leadership, but it is always good to talk things over with trusted people before you jump out of your box!

I am blessed to be part of a church where the spiritual leaders are godly people, and that has been so very important in my own ministry. My pastor and the elders of my church have always been supportive of my ministries at the church and on the radio. I have that home base of support and accountability and teaching, and that has been critically important in pursuing my passion. If I had forsaken my commitment to my church, I don't believe God would have blessed me.

Sign Number 6: God will give you the right people to help you.

God put some key people in my path to instruct me and help me. He has given me mentors and employees and donors and board members along the way, some popping up out of nowhere, to come alongside me and help me. It would take too many pages to tell you the many wonderful stories of how God brought the right people into my life at the right time.

Your passion will most likely involve others, and you'll need help and guidance. If it's a God-passion, those people will come your way.

Sign Number 7: You probably won't be qualified to do it.

That's a strange thing to say, isn't it? If God is trying to take you out of your box and move you into a new vision, most likely your first obstacle to overcome will be that you know how totally unqualified and inadequate you are to do it. I believe if you talk to any great Christian leaders or people who have done significant things for God's glory, they will all give you the same kind of response—they were not qualified to do what God has called them to do. The apostle Paul told us why this is true:

> But God chose the foolish things of the world to shame the wise; God chose the weak things of the world to shame the strong. He chose the lowly things of this world and the despised things—and the things that are not— to nullify the things that are, so that no one may boast before him. (1 Cor. 1:27-29)

If it were something that you could do in your own strength, who would get the glory for it? Getting out of your box and moving into unknown territory will be absolutely too much for you to do! So that's why God chose you, the apostle Paul writes. He chooses those who are not qualified, and then He equips them in ways they could never imagine, and He gets all the glory.

Your recognition of your inadequacy is the best thing you've got going for you, because it will force you to depend on God, to be humble, to be teachable, and you will always know it was all about God.

I am not suggesting that we can do our passion in any manner. It should always be done with a pursuit of excellence. And you may need further training or education before you can get going full-force. But, in many cases, the passion God gives us is so far above anything that we can achieve on our own, that it surprises us—and maybe others—to think that we would even attempt to do it.

It's a learning process.

Here are some of the things I've learned and am learning along the way as I've stepped out of my box to follow God's leading in my life.

- Not all of my bright ideas are God's passion for me.

- Some passions have a waiting period while God prepares me.

- Not everyone will share my passion and some people will discount it or try to discourage me.

- Perseverance is a large part of pursuing my passion.

- Passions take lots of hard work and there are some days when I wish I'd never had a passion. (But not many—not many!)

- Passions sometimes have a lifespan, a beginning and an ending, and I have to be sensitive to know when it's time to move on.

- When one passion dies, another comes along.

- A God-given passion is always a joy; it is fulfilling; it is in itself rewarding.

It really won't matter exactly what your passion is, because if it is a God-given passion, you will be passionate about it. And it won't matter to you if anybody else in the whole world recognizes it or not, as long as you can pursue that passion. It's burning inside of you and nothing else will satisfy you but to pursue that passion.

Remember this when it comes to pursuing your passion:

1. If you don't go for it, it will fade and you'll miss the blessing. Use it or lose it.

2. You will be held accountable to the Lord for the passions He has given to you. If you don't pursue

them, not only will you miss the blessing in this life, you'll miss the reward in eternity. You'll stand before Jesus at the Judgment Seat of Christ and He will recite the passion He had for you and want to know why you didn't pursue it. And you will be speechless, without excuse.

3. The more you pursue your passion, the more ability and gifts you will have to accomplish it. God is not going to waste talents on you if you're not going to use them. So He's waiting to see if you are serious about pursuing the passion He has put inside of you. If so, He will stretch you and gift you and equip you like you've never dreamed. But that won't happen until you put your oar in the water and start to row.

4. When you pursue your passion, your self-esteem issues will fade away. Frankly, you won't have much time to think about yourself, because a God-passion puts you in the middle of the lives of other people and you'll be too busy to worry too much about how you feel. However, you'll discover somewhere along the way that you feel better about yourself than you ever have, because in pursuing your passion, you'll find the fulfillment and success that has eluded you. It's a by-product of following God's will for you. It just happens when you pursue your passion.

5. When you pursue your passion, God will start working on polishing you to be the godly person He wants you to be. He won't let you stay in mediocrity. You will be forced to pray more, to study your Bible more, to get to know Jesus better than ever and to depend upon

Him more. It will lead you into a deeper and deeper relationship with the Lord. If that doesn't happen when you pursue your passion, question whether it is from the Lord or not. Or watch out; it will explode on you pretty soon because you'll be working in the power of your flesh instead of the power of God's Spirit. And that can only take you so far for so long.

Please, for the sake of the Kingdom of Christ and the glory due to Jesus Christ, get over putting yourself in some box that prevents you from the good works God has planned for you to do. When you get out of that box, you will move into the abundant life that Jesus promised for those who love Him.

Chapter Nine

Get Over
False Guilt

Feeling guilty is so common to most of us that a few years ago I wrote an entire book on the topic, entitled *Why Do I Always Feel Guilty?*[1] But how can I ignore the topic of false guilt in a book entitled *Get Over It*? I can't because false guilt is such a heavy, unnecessary burden and if you're carrying around that false guilt, I really want to help you get over it. You will be amazed at the freedom you will know when you can learn to put false guilt behind you.

What is false guilt?

False guilt is a guilt we impose upon ourselves. We allow it to take root in our minds, to start causing all kinds of bad feelings, to feed us all kinds of lies, which we begin to believe. Here are some examples of false guilt. It is:

---

1   *Why Do I Always Feel Guilty?* published by Harvest House Publishers, Copyright ©2007

- what we feel when we keep remembering what God has forgiven and forgotten!

- what we feel when someone appears to be disappointed in us

- what we feel when we have to say "no"

- what we feel when we try to please people and fail

- what we feel when we live with unrealistic expectations of ourselves

- what we feel when we allow others to dictate what and who we should be

- what we feel when we are unfairly accused of something

Notice that each one begins with "what we feel." It's a feeling, not grounded in truth, but nonetheless strong and real. Guilty feelings are very similar, whether they are true or false, and our challenge is to learn to discern the difference. We must learn to quickly analyze any guilt that comes our way: Is this true or false guilt? Have I done something that I can specifically identify for which I deserve blame? Or is this just that nebulous feeling of guilt I seem to get whenever I feel someone is unhappy with me, or I can't be superwoman or superman, or I struggle with something totally beyond my control.

Recently a wonderful young mom was lamenting the behavior of her four-year-old daughter. "She was so rebellious last night; she defied me in every way possible. She said terrible things to me. I finally put her to bed at 6:00. What have I done wrong? I try to teach her God's truth but it just looks like nothing is getting through to her. All my efforts to raise her to be kind and unselfish are not yielding any good results. She embarrassed me by her behavior and I just can't figure out what I'm doing wrong."

Is there a parent anywhere who hasn't taken on false guilt over a child, young or old, and blamed themselves for poor parenting while overlooking the fact that those children have a sinful nature and wills of their own, and parents truly are not to be held responsible for everything their children do? False guilt seems to haunt us as parents.

Another woman told me that her former husband went on a business trip, met a young woman who captured his fancy, and just that quickly, without any warning, came home to tell her that he didn't love her any longer and wanted a divorce. After over 20 years of marriage, he made an overnight decision to go for the young gal. And then he had the nerve to tell my friend, "You just weren't a good wife." She looked at me and said, "I thought I was a good wife, but I guess I wasn't."

Her husband blamed her for his affair and for the divorce, and she accepted the blame. That's false guilt, and I find that I easily take on false guilt when accused or confronted. If accused, I tend to respond with "guilty as charged," even when I'm not.

One of the first signs that you are dealing with false guilt is that you just can't pinpoint exactly why you feel guilty. It is a strong feeling that engulfs you and discourages you, but if you had to state why you feel guilty, you'd say things like, "Well, I just never seem to get it right," or "I don't know, I just should have known better," or "She's always telling me that I need to improve" or "I just can't seem to make anyone happy."

129

Notice how general those statements are. When you cannot pinpoint a specific reason for your guilt, it is highly likely you're dealing with false guilt.

Perhaps the false guilt we suffer from the most is guilt over our past. We all tend to go back and remember the sins of the past, and even though they are forgiven and God remembers them no longer, we don't seem to be able to purge our memory.

One night on my way home, I was tired and my mind was wandering, and my foot got heavy on the accelerator. I was going 45 in a 30-mile zone, and just two doors away from my own home, I got stopped for speeding and the nice officer wrote me a ticket.

As he handed it to me, he said that because I had a clean record, I could sign a paper asking for court supervision, pay my $50 fine, and the speeding ticket would not show up on my record at all. He said to me, "There will be no record anywhere of this offense; it will be as though it never happened."

That's what God does for us, but we don't have to pay $50. By simple faith and confession, He blots out our transgressions, and keeps no record of them. If you looked in His books, it wouldn't be there. Oh, how we need to understand this beautiful truth and learn to get over the guilt of forgiven sin, remembering there is therefore now no more condemnation for us who are in Christ Jesus. (See Romans 8:1)

During my ten-year hiatus from walking with the Lord, I had a friend with whom I worked, another single woman, and we were sharing a short vacation together in Florida. As she was driving us to the beach one day, a fourteen-wheel truck pulled into our lane and hit us head-on. The driver's seat took most of the impact, and my friend died shortly after she was taken to the hospital.

Not only did I not witness to her as I should have, but I failed to live a pure life and present a godly example to her. That is a terrible indication of my spiritual condition at that time, but it's been forgiven. I know from Scripture that my lack of witnessing did not determine her eternal destination; she made that choice and I pray she did make the choice to accept Jesus. How I wish I had shared my faith in Jesus with her; what a joy that would have been. But it is in the past, it is forgiven, it's no longer on the books against me, and I now refuse to allow it to plague my mind with guilt and regret. Obviously, I have not forgotten it; only God can purposely forget our sins—He alone has the ability to remember them no more. But I can still live free from the guilt of that past.

Determining the Source of Our Guilt

Much of our false guilt is from people who indicate their lack of satisfaction with us in some way. It is natural to feel guilty, but we need to check it out mentally every time it happens. When someone says, "Why weren't you ..." or "Why didn't you ..." and you immediately start to feel guilty, remind yourself that you may be dealing with false guilt.

I've had to learn to do this as I try to minister to people. I feel guilty when I don't have answers; when I can't come up with the right course of action and give them counsel that immediately makes them feel better or solves their problem. One woman who is desperately trying to put her marriage back together asked if I would help her husband find a good-paying job because she believes that financial stress is the main reason they are separated. My first reaction: *Mary, you should be able to help him find a job; she expects it of you.* But in a few seconds I was able to regain my senses, recognize false guilt, and lovingly explain that I really don't have that ability.

Once I was speaking at a seminar, and a woman came up to say that she was so disappointed because I didn't talk about empty nesters. Immediately I started to feel guilty because I had disappointed her, but very quickly I did a mental retake and just reminded myself that God had not laid it on my heart to talk about the problems of empty nesters. I don't even know what I would say about it, and I can't feel guilty because I didn't meet her specific need. I can't meet everyone's needs, but I don't have to feel guilty about that.

Recently a woman stopped me in church to ask for help in dealing with a teenage daughter, one who is rebellious and has a difficult relationship with her mother. She was looking for a seminar on that topic. Since I am director of women's ministries at my church, I want to be able to help any woman who comes to me on any particular topic. But I could not find what she wanted—a seminar for mothers with rebellious teenage daughters.

My first reaction was to blame myself. I thought *Why haven't you had a seminar on this topic? If you were doing your job as director of women's ministries, then you could meet her need.* It's that ever-present tendency to feel guilty when I cannot meet someone else's expectations. Having many years of experience with this kind of false guilt, I am learning to recognize it much more quickly now and refuse to allow it to move into my thought life any further.

I did find some books to recommend to her, and when I called to share that information with her, she seemed very appreciative that I had responded to her. As I hung up the phone, I thought about how pleased she seemed to be that I had at least tried. She wasn't dumping guilt on me. I believe that much of our false guilt is self-imposed. We imagine that others are blaming us, even when they are not.

Learning to Manage False Guilt

Not long ago, a friend confronted me with something I had said which had hurt her feelings. Obviously I was very sorry to hear that my words had caused her some pain and, of course, I apologized and accepted full responsibility. But I can tell you that I did not feel guilty about it. The reason was that my intentions and motivations were pure; there was no malice or ill-feelings or desire in my heart to do harm and, in fact, I simply thought it was a clever and funny comment.

Why didn't I feel guilty? I was guilty of hurting her feelings, but as soon as it was brought to my attention, I apologized and then privately I prayed for understanding of why my words had caused pain when they were never intended that way. The Lord graciously revealed to me that I have to be careful with "quips." I can easily come back with a quip without thinking about how it might sound to someone else. (I think it's a result of being raised with brothers and spending most of my professional life with men, who use quips and barbs as a way of showing fondness and friendship. But that's not true with women.)

So I've begun to pray about that and the Spirit of God has checked my spirit several times since then, reminding me to keep that quip to myself. I am grateful for the experience, because it has increased my sensitivity to others and helped me to make some needed changes, but I don't carry guilt over it because I had no bad intentions— just the opposite.

If this had happened some years earlier in my life, I would have lost many nights of sleep over it. I would have allowed the guilt to saturate my mind and my emotions for days or weeks. I would have relived it time and again, probably done some mental shifting of blame, and may have allowed it to cause a rift in our relationship. None of those things happened this time, because I'm learning to deal with false guilt.

The first and most important step in learning to manage false guilt is to recognize it. We must develop the practice of examining our guilty feelings and determining if they are true or false. That will do more than anything else to rid your mind of false guilt, because once you know the guilt is not deserved, it's much easier to put it out of your mind.

The second step is to replace wrong thinking with right thinking. When you're dealing with false guilt, you must, by choice, or by a set of your will, push that wrong thinking out of your mind. I emphasize "by a set of your will" because your feelings will take you in another direction. This is done by faith and in obedience to Scripture.

One way to do this is through praise to the Lord. Start counting your blessings. Begin thanking God for the good things in your life. Refuse to allow the thoughts of false guilt to have a place in your mind.

There Is No Condemnation!

I love this passage from Romans 8:33-34, from Phillips' *The New Testament in Modern English*:

Who would dare to accuse us, whom God has chosen? The judge himself has declared us free from sin. Who is in a position to condemn? Only Christ, and Christ died for us, Christ rose for us, Christ reigns in power for us, Christ prays for us!

Only Christ is qualified to accuse us of wrong, and after we become Christians, He doesn't! Do we have a right to condemn ourselves if Jesus doesn't condemn us? Can anyone else truly condemn you, if Jesus doesn't?

To condemn someone is, in today's vernacular, to "lay a guilt trip" on them. Substituting that phrase for the word "condemn," this passage would read:

Who would dare to accuse us, whom God has chosen? The judge himself has declared us free from sin. Who is in a position **to lay a guilt trip on us**? Only Christ, and Christ died for us, Christ rose for us, Christ reigns in power for us, Christ prays for us!

To allow ourselves to wallow in false guilt is to live in condemnation. It is the devil's trick, and I can imagine that God must shake His head at those of us who are His children and yet continue to live under the burden of false guilt.

Remember, if God is not condemning you, you have no right to let anyone else condemn you—not even yourself. I would urge you to memorize Romans 8:1: "Therefore, there is now no condemnation for those who are in Christ Jesus," and Isaiah 43:25: "I, even I, am he who blots out your transgressions, for my own sake, and remembers your sins no more."

Remember that you can get over false guilt and declare you are no longer under its power. It may be a bit of a journey to learn to manage that false guilt, and you may experience both success and failure as you head down that path, but don't be discouraged. There is great relief ahead as we stand firm in the freedom that Christ gives us, and refuse to allow ourselves to be burdened again by a yoke of slavery, as Galatians 5:1 admonishes us.

Chapter Ten

Get Over
Your Discontent
with Singleness

Perhaps because I myself am single, this topic seems important to me. With over thirty years in ministry, both in my church and through my radio program, I know that being discontent with being single is widespread, especially in Christian circles. This is common to men as well as women, and when it is out of control it affects a person's life in the most harmful ways. I've counseled countless numbers of women—and some men—on this topic, and in addition, this is one area where I can say, "I've been there and done that." So I address this topic with a lot of empathy and some wisdom that comes from years of hindsight.

God designed and instituted marriage; He is the author of sexual relationships and desire. And within His design, marriage and all that goes with it are to be honored and held in high esteem. It's no wonder that most people—

especially in their young adult lives—deeply desire to be married, have children, and establish a good family. Those are God-given desires and there is no need to deny those desires or feel guilty about them. So you want to be married some day? No problem. You don't have to get over that.

However, when that desire becomes an obsession, as it so often does, so that every part of your life is colored by this underlying and overwhelming desire to be married, then you need to get over that restless, discontented feeling; that gnawing lie which keeps nagging at your mind and telling you that life cannot be really good or totally fulfilling until and unless you marry. The enemy of our soul, Satan, loves to find ways to keep us discontented, because then our effectiveness in Kingdom work is decreased.

This extreme discontent with singleness is like a black cloud that spoils every other thing in your life. It diminishes the joy of success in careers or other friendships or even ministry involvement. The ten years I spent desperately searching for someone to marry me were like a roller-coaster ride. When there was hope that the current relationship might indeed materialize into marriage, I was riding high. When those hopes were dashed or non-existent, I was at the bottom. Regardless of the success I had in my career, which was not insignificant, or the wonderful friendships I had or the supportive family members in my life, my discontent with being single overshadowed it all. I learned to put on a "happy face" and cover up so that few people knew the turmoil within me, but believe me, it hardly ever left my mind and very few days passed when I was not mentally and emotionally obsessed with it.

I often feel frustrated when trying to encourage a single person to believe that singleness is not a fate worse than death! Indeed it can be a time of great freedom and adventure, an avenue to fulfillment and excitement. It seems like my words just bounce off the person I'm talking to and no matter how eloquent or convincing I may be or how much Scripture I quote, it doesn't penetrate into their thought processes. I remember talking to a young twenty-something woman, who admitted she wanted to be married and could not believe that her life could ever be anything good unless she was married. I asked her if she was willing to give God permission to change her attitude toward marriage, and she could not believe that even God could change her. Furthermore, she didn't want to run the risk that He might!

Somehow it seems that "getting over" an obsession to be married doesn't come easily for any of us and it is an issue that has to be confronted more than once—indeed, many times throughout our years of singleness. But I know from my own experience and that of many other wonderful single adults I know that we indeed have a choice as to whether our discontent with being single will continue to rule our lives—to ruin our lives—or not. Once again, this is a choice we make as to what we think about singleness, how much we think about it, and how well we learn to bring those obsessive thoughts into captivity and make them obedient to Christ. It is just so true that the problem here lies in our thought lives.

What the Bible Says About Singleness

First Corinthians 7 is seldom used for sermon material. It doesn't fit in too well with this common idea that God intended marriage for everyone and anything else is second best. Here are verses 32 to 35 from that chapter:

I would like you to be free from concern. An unmarried man is concerned about the Lord's affairs—how he can please the Lord. But a married man is concerned about the affairs of this world—how he can please his wife—and his interests are divided. An unmarried woman or virgin is concerned about the Lord's affairs: Her aim is to be devoted to the Lord in both body and spirit. But a married woman is concerned about the affairs of this world—how she can please her husband. I am saying this for your own good, not to restrict you, but that you may live in a right way in undivided devotion to the Lord.

Often people say to me, "I don't understand how you do all the things you do. Where do you find the time?" I am able to do all the things I do to a great extent because I'm single. I don't have to worry about having a meal on the table each evening. I can get up early and stay up late without upsetting anybody's schedule or hurting anyone's feelings. There's a freedom in my singleness which, if used correctly, can give me more time for ministry than I would have otherwise.

Now, I also recognize that I miss out on many joys and pleasures shared by two people who are married. There is a loneliness to cope with at times, and that feeling which sometimes creeps in to remind you you're not the most important person in the world to some one person.

Yes, there are pluses and minuses, assets and liabilities. But what we singles forget is that's true of the other side of the fence too. There are negative aspects to marriage, even a good marriage. I can assure you that many happily married people look at my freedom with some envy at times.

The key thing we need to understand is that God has not advocated one lifestyle—marriage—as the number-one, normal way to live, and the other lifestyle—singleness—as second best, leftovers for those who missed the marriage boat for some reason or another.

Let me remind you of some people in Scripture who were either certainly or most likely single: Jesus, the apostle Paul, Mary, Martha and Lazarus, Lydia, Mary Magdalene, Dorcas. Many others have no reference to marriage and have lifestyles that would lead you to think they were probably single, including some of the disciples and many in the early church.

There are some dangers in allowing ourselves to think that marriage is the only normal lifestyle and it will solve all our problems. First of all, you place an unduly heavy responsibility and expectation on marriage, which it will not be able to live up to. You're setting yourself up for disappointment and failure if and when you do get married.

Secondly, you're asking too much of that other person who will be your mate if and when you do marry. Even if you marry the most wonderful person in the world, he or she will not be able to meet your needs totally. To expect so much is to invite disaster.

Thirdly, when a person is consumed with the desire to be married, they usually become less and less attractive because they are unconsciously transmitting that message through body language, facial expressions, conversation, etc. It's an unappealing perfume that exudes from every pore, and you can smell it a mile off!

Fourthly, when we think that marriage is an essential, we start to make an idol out of it. It becomes more important to us than anything else. That's idolatry, and God simply does not tolerate idolatry in our lives. Any desire, even a legitimate one, can become an idol. And when that desire is out of control, several other telltale symptoms usually accompany it, such as:

- Emotional highs and lows, depending upon whether there's a prospect on the scene or not.

- Decreased spiritual emphasis. Not much time in God's Word or prayer. Not much desire to talk about spiritual things.

- Minimal outreach to others. Little involvement in other people's problems. Lack of awareness of when others are hurting.

- Exaggerated concern about looks and appearance.

Well, what do we do? Throw up our hands and quit? Leave the human race? Put our heads in the sand and ignore? Join the nearest monastery? Pray for the gift of celibacy?

None of the above. We go back to Matthew 6:33 and practice it: "But seek first his kingdom and his righteousness, and all these things will be given to you as well." Does that verse say we'll get our marriage partner if we seek first God's kingdom? No, it says we'll get what we need, and God knows what we need better than we do.

If you're a single person who struggles with this mistaken attitude toward marriage, you're the only one who can change that. Society won't help you; the church can't do it for you; your family may never change their view. But you can change, if you recognize the error in your thinking and start programing your mind to think biblically.

I did not say you would lose your desire to be married, but rather that you would not be consumed by it. You'll know there is purpose and meaning in what you're doing as a single person. The thought of never being married won't send you into a panic attack.

I trust you'll go to God in prayer concerning your attitude toward marriage, and ask for His perspective. When we see things through God's eyes, what a difference it makes. As Christian singles, we have God's power to give us consistent victory in this area.

Here are some practical things we can do to get over our obsessive discontent with being single.

• Find substitute relationships and activities

While men and women were created for each other and God recognized that we needed this type of relationship, it is not the only satisfying relationship we can have. For those of you who are waiting and hoping to be married, ask God to give you another kind of relationship that will fill some of those needs for you and where you can do the same for that other person.

Jonathan and David in Scripture had that kind of friendship. Mary and Martha were two sisters who were evidently never married and found companionship in each other and their brother. No doubt the disciples developed very close friendships as they traveled and ministered with Jesus. Friendships are essential parts of our lives that can bring great meaning and joy. A person who is obsessed with finding a marriage partner may neglect his or her friendships and miss the wonderful value that they offer. Proverbs 18:24 (KJV) says, "A man that hath friends must shew himself friendly: and there is a friend that sticketh closer than a brother." That kind of friend is a great treasure, and to find that kind of friend we have to be that kind of friend.

• Give of yourself to others

This is one of the most important biblical principles to put into practice in your life, and when you do, you're going to discover how much easier it is to deal with your singleness.

I think of Karen, a dear, lovely single woman who is a speech therapist for a local school board. She is continually giving herself to others, sharing her life with others, doing things for others. Karen is being used by God to touch many people in many ways. I seriously doubt that she has much time to feel sorry for herself or feel left out. I can think of many married people who live much lonelier lives than Karen.

Would she like to find a life-mate some day? My guess is she would. She's as "normal as blueberry pie." But I've never heard her complain about it. It isn't the first topic of conversation when you get near her. She is not consumed with her singleness. She's too busy sending eternal treasures ahead of her to heaven by investing her time in other people.

There are many, many single Christians like Karen. When you give of yourself to others, you die to your own self and that's when you find life! It certainly has been true in my life. After spending ten years self-absorbed with the desire to find a husband, the last thirty years have been spent in service and ministry. And there's no comparison as to my happiness and contentment between the two periods of my life. I am convinced that staying busily involved in God's work, reaching out to other people and focusing on their needs instead of mine has made all the difference in the world.

• Control your thinking and your words

Please be careful how you allow yourself to think and talk about being single. When you find yourself thinking those self-pity single thoughts, bring those thoughts into captivity. They are not true or noble or lovely or of a good report and, according to Philippians 4:8, you're not allowed to think them.

When you find yourself talking about the difficulty of finding a Christian mate, or moaning and groaning about being single and having to do everything yourself, etc., etc., stop right in the middle of those words and speak words that edify and encourage you as well as others. And don't listen to those discouraging words from your friends.

Often messages to singles center around this theme: *When you're everything God wants you to be, when you've learned to be content right where you are, when you are attractive enough and spiritual enough, then you'll be worthy of a mate and he or she will come right along.* That's not biblically accurate. God doesn't reward us with a mate for spiritual maturity! And furthermore our motivation to be a godly person should never be to try to manipulate God to give us what we want. Obviously, some very godly people never marry; I could name so many of them. And many people who are a long way from maturity in Christ find what often looks like wonderful partners at an early age.

Some single Christian adults live in guilt and frustration as they struggle to be good enough to have a husband or wife—thin enough, spiritual enough, pretty enough, talented enough, etc., etc., etc. This is warped and wrong thinking. We need to be consumed with a desire to be a godly woman or man because the Bible tells us to be, because we love Jesus, because we want to please Him, because we know that when we give Him control, the best things happen in our lives. We should want to look and be our best because He deserves our best. When our motivation is otherwise, it is not pure.

One final thought: Everyone will be single in heaven. Jesus said so:

> At the resurrection people will neither marry nor be given in marriage; they will be like the angels in heaven. (Matt. 22:30)

So for all eternity we'll not be married to other people, but we will be the Bride of Christ. If you live to be one hundred, how many more years do you have on this earth? Is it fifty or seventy or eighty—or fifteen or ten? It really doesn't matter what the number is because compared to eternity it is infinitesimal—so small you can't measure it. So you may or may not live out the rest of these earthly years as a single person. Does it really matter that much in light of eternity? I truly hope you will ask God to help you get over your exaggerated and desperate desire to be married, and enjoy the great things He wants to do for you and through you while you are single.

Chapter Eleven

Get Over
Your Fear of
Trusting God

As I've already described, I spent many years "doing my own thing," as we say, not obedient to God's voice in my life. Though God in His graciousness has turned those ashes into beauty (Isa. 61:3), how I wish I had not wasted those precious years which are gone forever. As I look back with God's perspective on that time, I now recognize that the underlying problem in those ten years was that I was afraid to trust God with control of my life. I was actually fearful of allowing the God of the universe to run my show. I shake my head now and wonder how I could have been so stupid for so long.

So many of us hang on to the controls of our lives, afraid to trust God, as if to say that we know what's better for us than God does, and we are more trustworthy than He is. Of course, we don't think those thoughts; we just live our lives that way. It truly shocked me to discover this in myself; for had you asked me during those ten years if I trusted God, I would have emphatically answered yes. Self-deception is just that—we are deceived and when we are deceived, we don't know it! That's the nature of deception. As soon as you know you've been deceived, you are no longer.

As I close this book—which hopefully encourages you to "get over" things that are holding you down and keeping you from freedom and joy—my prayer is that if you have been fearful of trusting God, you will recognize it maybe for the first time, and you will recognize the foolishness and sinfulness of your fear of trusting God.

While my particular fear of trusting God was evidenced in my fear of being single, the root cause of that was because I didn't really believe that God's plan for my life could be better than my own. Your fear of God may be revealed in quite different symptoms: *You're afraid of not having enough money to support your lifestyle or fund your retirement. You're afraid of not achieving your career goals. You're afraid of being rejected. You're afraid of losing the approval of someone or some ones.* Whatever your fear of the future is—and it is always a fear of what might or might not happen—its root cause is that you really are afraid to let go of the controls of your life and simply trust God's plan to be a good plan.

I remember well the sleepless night when I finally said, "God, I'll do anything you ask of me, if only you will give me peace. I'll even be single forever." Hesitatingly, I finally exercised a little bit of faith and told God I was willing to trust Him. It became clear to me that He couldn't possibly do a worse job at running my life than I was doing!

That little bit of weak faith on my part was the beginning of learning to trust God. Through weeks and months of pain, as I watched my hopes and dreams die, He replaced those broken dreams with Himself. In the intervening years, I have learned to trust Him more and more, and know the joy and peace of His fellowship. And I testify to you today that God is trustworthy. Furthermore, He's infinitely better at running your life than you are!

Now that I see the marvelous changes in my life, I ask myself why I did not trust Him sooner. And the answer that comes back is that I did not really understand who God is, and therefore how trustworthy He is. Though I had been taught the basics of Christianity from my earliest days and had graduated from a Christian college, the knowledge of God's trustworthiness had somehow not gone from my head to my heart.

Believing the Basics

I want to share with you the three basic truths about God that changed my life, as I began to really understand them. They are simple beyond belief. Undoubtedly, most of you will nod your head in agreement with them. But if you truly believe them, those fears of trusting God have to go.

1. **Learning to trust God begins by reminding ourselves of His character and power, and then asking ourselves if we really believe God is who He says He is.**

Here are just a few verses that describe the nature of God: Isaiah 44:6 tells us our **God is the only God**:

> This is what the LORD says—Israel's King and Redeemer, the LORD Almighty: I am the first and I am the last; apart from me there is no God.

Verse 24 tells us that **He is God the Creator:**

> This is what the LORD says—your Redeemer, who formed
> you in the womb: I am the Lord, who has made all things,
> who alone stretched out the heavens, who spread out
> the earth by myself.

Our God is all-powerful and does what He pleases.

> I know that the LORD is great, that our LORD is greater
> than all gods. The LORD does whatever pleases him, in
> the heavens and on the earth, in the seas and all their
> depths. (Ps. 135:5-6)

He is holy and perfect, and does not make mistakes.

> He is the Rock, his works are perfect, and all his ways are
> just. A faithful God who does no wrong, upright and just
> is he. (Deut. 32:4)

This is basic theology that any Christian would claim to
believe, but there is a huge difference in knowing the
theology and believing it to the extent that it affects us. Too
often we've become so accustomed to hearing these basic
truths that we don't even stop to consider their impact. Step
one in getting over your fear of trusting God is to affirm
in your soul that He is the only true God, the Creator of
everything, who has all power and never makes a mistake.
And for this to become a part of your very being, you need
to remind yourself daily of these basic truths, repeat them
out loud to yourself, write them on a card and put them in
front of your face as often as possible. It is truth that sets us
free, and this truth needs to be our daily bread.

When I was making my journey back from my broken
dream and started a pursuit to get to know God better,

I began a prayer journal where I wrote down the many attributes of God. And each day I would use that list at the beginning of my prayer time, praising God for who He was—the entire Trinity, God the Father, God the Son, and God the Holy Spirit—reciting out loud and thanking God for each of those attributes on my list. I added to that list as new attributes of God were revealed to me through Scripture, and it became a long list of several pages. I am convinced that my daily repetition of the attributes of God in praise was the linchpin that changed my thinking and set me free from the fear of trusting God. No one ever advised me to do this; I just somehow realized it was important. (Could be the Holy Spirit had a part in it!)

Later I read this quote from William Law, a British theologian who lived from 1686 to 1761, and realized the same Holy Spirit had instructed him to do the same thing. I have written it in my journal. The language is antiquated but the truth is important:

> When you begin your petitions, use such various expressions of the attributes of God, as may make you most sensible of the greatness and power of the Divine Nature ... For these representations of the Divine attributes, which show us in some degree the majesty and greatness of God, are an excellent means of raising our hearts into lively acts of worship and adoration ... For such representations, which describe so many characteristics of our Saviour's nature and power, are not only proper acts of adoration, but will, if they are repeated with any attention, fill our hearts with the highest fervour of true devotion.

2. Knowing God's Personal Care

Assuming we have assimilated those basic truths, the next important issue is to understand how this same God feels about us. After all, we are but specks in a great mass of humanity and in a vast universe. Do we make any difference to God? Again, Scripture gives us an answer.

God does not lose track of you!

Why do you say, O Jacob, and complain, O Israel, "My way is hidden from the Lord, my cause is disregarded by my God?" Do you not know? Have you not heard? The Lord is the everlasting God, the Creator of the ends of the earth. He will not grow tired or weary, and his understanding no one can fathom. (Isa. 40:27-28)

God knows you intimately.

Are not two sparrows sold for a penny? Yet not one of them will fall to the ground outside your Father's care. And even the very hairs of your head are all numbered. So don't be afraid; you are worth more than many sparrows. (Matt. 10:29-31)

Look at the birds of the air; they do not sow or reap or store away in barns, and yet your heavenly Father feeds them. Are you not much more valuable than they? (Matt. 6:26)

You have searched me, LORD, and you know me. You know when I sit and when I rise; you perceive my thoughts from afar. You discern my going out and my lying down; you are familiar with all my ways. Before a word is on my tongue you, LORD, know it completely. (Ps. 139:1-4)

Nothing can separate you from His love.

> For I am convinced that neither death nor life, neither angels nor demons, neither the present nor the future, nor any powers, neither height nor depth, nor anything else in all creation, will be able to separate us from the love of God that is in Christ Jesus our Lord. (Rom. 8:38-39)

These Scriptures, as well as many others, clearly state that the God we worship, the one and only God, the eternal God, the God of all power, wisdom, and holiness—this very God really cares about you and me with a care and concern unsurpassed by any other person in the world.

3. God's Plans Are Always Best

Then, if we accept those basic truths, they have to lead us to this third and most important conclusion: God's plans for us are always superior to any other plans. If you believe God is God and He cares for you, then you cannot logically deny this truth: God is smarter than you are at running your life. Therefore, you can trust Him. Not only *can* you trust Him, but it is the only logical thing to do. Nothing else makes any sense.

Just look at what the Scriptures tell us about God's intentions toward us:

> No good thing does he withhold from those whose walk is blameless. (Ps. 84:11b)

> Now to him who is able to do immeasurably more than all we ask or imagine, according to his power that is at work within us. (Eph. 3:20)

> Fear the LORD, you his saints, for those who fear him lack nothing. The lions may grow weak and hungry, but those who seek the LORD lack no good thing. (Ps. 34:9-10)

> "For I know the plans I have for you," declares the Lord, "plans to prosper you and not to harm you, plans to give you hope and a future." (Jer. 29:11)

The irrefutable, logical conclusion is clear. There simply can be no middle ground. If we believe with our hearts, not just our heads, that God is God, eternal, all-powerful, holy and perfect, and that this very God cares for us more than any earthly being could ever care, and that His plans for our lives are far better than anything we could maneuver on our own, we have to get over our fear of trusting Him. He can be nothing but trustworthy. He will lead us into the best paths. To fail to relinquish the control of our lives to Him would be foolhardy and disastrous.

I am beginning to realize what arrogance it is on my part to refuse to trust God. To fail to trust Him at every turn in my life is a grave and serious sin. It is pride at its very worse.

Comprehending how totally trustworthy God is leads us to yield to His total lordship in our lives. And we learn to yield more and more as we get to know Him better. This takes the monkey off our backs! It gives us a marvelous freedom, because we are no longer responsible for managing our own destinies. Someone far more qualified is now in charge—the God of all the ages—and we can be absolutely sure that whatever He asks of us will be the best thing for us.

Whatever the fear that is keeping you from trusting God, it is unfounded and unreasonable, and it is a trick of Satan to keep you from the joy and peace of a trusting, yielded life. Let go of those fears today, confess your sin of unbelief, get into God's Word daily and get to know God better, and you, too, can get over your fear of trusting God.

POSTSCRIPT

In Romans 12:8, Paul identifies mercy as one of the spiritual gifts and says, "if it is showing mercy, let him do it cheerfully." My colleagues on staff with me at my church often remind me—in good fun—that I don't have the gift of mercy. I've confessed it myself, for I know it is a fact! I'm so thankful for the people of God who have this gift. They are compassionate, sympathetic, patient saints who cannot help but reach out and help those in need, whether it is a physical, emotional, financial, or spiritual need.

But one thing I'm learning in this journey with Jesus is that lack of any spiritual gift is not a license to disobey, nor an excuse for lack of love. I may not have the gift of mercy but God expects me to be merciful, and I really want to be. So, although the title of this book might appear to be a "tough love" approach to the issues I've covered, truly with all my heart I desire to see others move forward so they can know the abundant life Jesus came to give us.

The joy of serving Jesus Christ is second to nothing else, and I'm praying that as you have read these chapters, you've learned a pathway to move on from what has kept you mired in a mudhole or two.

I fully understand that there is no instant, one-time fix for setting us free from these "mudholes," but we have to start somewhere, don't we? We have to find a handle on truth that we can grab on to and hang on for dear life as God the Holy Spirit changes us from the inside out and we truly are then able to live in the freedom Jesus has purchased for us. It is for freedom that Christ has set us free; we must stand firm in that freedom so that we are no longer burdened by a yoke of slavery (Gal. 5:1).

So, as you close this book, having made it all the way through, I just want you to know that I believe God's Spirit has led you to read it and, therefore, He desires to set you free from whatever is weighing you down—to help you get over whatever that is. He has good plans for you and good works for you to do, and you don't want to miss them!

You are welcome to contact me at:

tcww@christianworkingwoman.org.

Extraordinary Women by Grace
Stories of Women like you

MARY WHELCHEL

6 women from Jesus' family line in the Bible, 6 women from Jesus' family today in the Church - all ordinary yet all extraordinary!

As you read about these ordinary women, you will see how God's extraordinary grace was extended to:

ISBN 978-1-84550-176-1

- Fran's dysfunctional family
- Mary's humble beginnings and lack of education
- Judy's wrong choices and illicit relationships
- Pam's illegitimacy and abuse as a child
- Tamar's victimization by the system
- Camille's sordid history with men

Mary Whelchel's conversational style, honed from successful broadcasting, make these stories of biblical and contemporary women linger in your thoughts - bringing you face-to-face with the life-changing power of God's grace.

You'll discover that God transformed ordinary women in the past – and continues to do so today. *Extraordinary Women by Grace* offers hope and encouragement to all women, regardless of past failures, defeats, or missed opportunities.

Christian Focus Publications

Our mission statement –

STAYING FAITHFUL

In dependence upon God we seek to impact the world through literature faithful to His infallible Word, the Bible. Our aim is to ensure that the Lord Jesus Christ is presented as the only hope to obtain forgiveness of sin, live a useful life and look forward to heaven with Him.

Our books are published in four imprints:

CHRISTIAN
FOCUS

Popular works including biographies, commentaries, basic doctrine and Christian living.

CHRISTIAN
HERITAGE

Books representing some of the best material from the rich heritage of the church.

MENTOR

Books written at a level suitable for Bible College and seminary students, pastors, and other serious readers. The imprint includes commentaries, doctrinal studies, examination of current issues and church history.

CF4•K

Children's books for quality Bible teaching and for all age groups: Sunday school curriculum, puzzle and activity books; personal and family devotional titles, biographies and inspirational stories – because you are never too young to know Jesus!

Christian Focus Publications Ltd,
Geanies House, Fearn, Ross-shire,
IV20 1TW, Scotland, United Kingdom.
www.christianfocus.com